Advai
Only 10

D0627974

"*Only 10 Seconds to Care* can
patients and improve how c.   .... care. We
support Dr. Harpham's efforts to advocate for patients so they
can live life on their own terms. By sharing these stories of survivorship, Dr. Harpham is empowering people with information
that can benefit them personally and offering valuable lessons for
ways we can effect change in our healthcare system." — *Doug
Ulman, President/CEO, Lance Armstrong Foundation*

"Accessible, insightful, and compassionate . . . .With gentle
humor and tough love, Wendy Harpham takes doctors and
patients by the hand and teaches them how to build a potential-
ly life-saving bridge between the human being in the white coat
and the human being in the paper smock. I'll be recommending
this book to every survivor I know and handing a copy to my
oncologist at our next visit." — *Joni Rodgers, author of* BALD IN
THE LAND OF BIG HAIR

"Wendy Harpham's multiple perspectives—physician, patient,
fellow-traveler—exemplify how having an open heart, a listening
ear, and respect for the human being who is our patient heals not
only our patients but ourselves." — *Diane Meier, MD, Professor of
Geriatrics, Internal Medicine, and the Catherine Gaisman Professor of
Medical Ethics at the Mount Sinai School of Medicine*

"Wendy Harpham teaches us how to communicate with our
patients as they navigate their illness and its treatments. We will
all walk that road. Today a doctor, tomorrow a patient. She lets
us know that surviving is not an absolute but a relative state.
'Help your patients make the most of it…Listen carefully…Be
there.' These are just a few of Wendy's messages that will help
us heal and comfort." — *Ronald Levy, MD, Professor and Chief,
Division of Oncology at Stanford University Medical Center*

"Wendy Harpham's book will be useful to students embarking
on their initial clinical experiences. Weaving [Dr. Harpham's]
own experience as a patient into the issues provides a unique
view that is all the more valuable. I was especially impressed

with her handling of 'hope' with patients; the three stories explicitly addressing this difficult issue are among the best I have seen on the subject." — *Joseph V. Simone, MD, Director, University of Florida-Shands Cancer Center*

"Wendy Harpham speaks to healthcare providers about the importance of caring, but most importantly, what caring looks like. She interprets situations from the patient perspective, pointing out potential barriers to communication between the patient and clinicians. By taking time to care, clinicians will gain a better understanding of the patient as an individual that will enable them to provide care that is truly patient specific." — *Winnie Kittiko, RN, MS*

"Everyone can learn something new . . . including patients! In *Only 10 Seconds to Care*, Wendy Harpham shows us that a quality patient encounter need not be hampered by time. She gives us practical tools that illustrate how well-selected words and perceptive listening skills can lead to respectful and productive interactions." — *Susan Leigh, RN, Oncology Nurse and Cancer Survivor*

"Wendy Harpham moves seamlessly between patient and physician sides of medical encounters, offering gentle and useful advice to physicians about how much caring can happen in literally 10 seconds. Dr. Harpham's use of her illness experiences to teach her medical colleagues what patient are feeling is a gift to the medical profession." — *Arthur W. Frank, author of* THE RENEWAL OF GENEROSITY: ILLNESS, MEDICINE, AND HOW TO LIVE

"Given the reality of today's busy and stressful healthcare environment, Dr. Harpham's message is timely for all healthcare professionals, whether novice or expert, and in any specialty. Her suggestions on what to say or do are practical and easily integrated into daily encounters. As the book's title suggests, caring is possible in brief moments – and this book can be read in brief moments – reminding us of the importance of the clinician-patient bond." — *Brenda Nevidjon, MSN, RN, FAAN, President, Oncology Nursing Society, Clinical Professor, Duke University School of Nursing.*

Praise for Wendy Harpham

DIAGNOSIS: CANCER. A GUIDE TO THE FIRST MONTHS OF HEALTHY SURVIVORSHIP

"...Harpham provides clear, simple but comprehensive and compassionate answers and esplanations to ease [patients' and their families'] concerns and help them make the best possible decisions about everything from choosing treatments to coping with feelings, family and friends. This book —the very best of its kind—should be a bible for everyone facing cancer." — *Jane E. Brody, personal health columnist,* THE NEW YORK TIMES

"Wendy Harpham is an inspiration to all touched by cancer. Her solid advice and upbeat perspective are invaluable." — *Diane Blum, MSW, executive director, Cancer Care, Inc.*

HAPPINESS IN A STORM: FACING ILLNESS AND EMBRACING LIFE AS A HEALTHY SURVIVOR

"Consoling, personal, humorous, hopeful. . . *Happiness in a Storm* is a lifeboat for cancer survivrs. Wendy Harpham's book is all about saving the quality of lives for patients and families facing any illness or injury." — *Kathleen M. Foley, MD, attending neurologist in Pain and Palliative Care Service, Memorial Sloan-Kettering Cancer Center*

"Dr. Wendy Harpham is a pioneer in the art and science of being alive. With a huge heart, scalpel-sharp wit, hard-won wisdom, and uncompromising clarity, *Happiness in a Storm* transcends the usual chicken soup, steering the course toward a stronger, more joyful life." — *Joni Rodgers, author of* BALD IN THE LAND OF BIG HAIR

WHEN A PARENT HAS CANCER: A GUIDE TO CARING FOR YOUR CHILDREN

"Through honest, gutsy, yet innocent windows, Dr. Harpham lets us see that 'happily ever after' can become 'happier...even after.' " — *Judy Gerner, Director, Anderson Network, MD Anderson Cancer Center, University of Texas*

"...few [books] have come close to capturing the realistic experience of being a parent with cancer and the extraordinary implications that this diagnosis has for children they love....Dr. Harpham has given all parents diagnosed with cancer bountiful, practical advice on how to cope and even thrive in their relationship with their children. She has bestowed a gift to all of us with this exceptional publication." — *Ellen Stovall, Executive Director, National Coalition for Cancer Survivorship.*

AFTER CANCER: A GUIDE TO YOUR NEW LIFE

"The magic of survival can be challenged by the vast unknown and potential problems of life beyond cancer therapy. Finally, a book has been written that validates these issues, offers practical advice to resolve problems, and impels survivors to flourish after adversity." —*Susan Leigh, RN, President, National Coalition for Cancer Survivorship*

"A timely and marvelously practical book on a topic too long neglected. Every page reflects the author's unmatchable credentials: her struggles as a patient, her expertise as a physician, her writing skill, her sensitive caring, her passion for honesty and overcoming. A must-read book for cancer survivors and family members, and a must-use book for caregiver professionals." — *Harold Y. Vanderpool, PhD, ThM, Institute for the Medical Humanities, University of Texas Medical Branch, Galveston*

Only
10 Seconds
to Care

Help and Hope
for Busy Clinicians

WENDY SCHLESSEL HARPHAM, MD, FACP

ACP Press®

American College of Physicians   Philadelphia

Editorial Coordinator: Angela Gabella
Composition and interior design by Michael Ripca,
  ACP Graphic Services
Cover design by Lisa Torrieri, ACP Graphic Services
Printing/binding by Versa Press
Printed in the United States of America

ISBN: 978-1-934465-39-4

09 10 11 12 13 / 10 9 8 7 6 5 4 3 2 1

For my friend, Susan Lee Shapiro,
who shares my love of words

Acknowledgments

I am—and will be forever—grateful for the efforts of everyone who helps me help others. Many people have been involved with this book at its various stages:

- Ted, my dedicated and selfless husband, who has continued to help me work my way through the challenge of saying what I mean.

- Serena Stockwell, my editor at *Oncology Times,* who invited me to write a regular column, "View from the Other Side of the Stethoscope," and has given me the time and space to explore these topics.

- Faith Hamlin, my literary agent, who has gone beyond the call of duty.

- Tom Hartman and the staff at ACP Press, who produced this book in record time.

- Susan Lee Shapiro, who has poured over every single word and punctuation mark.

- My friends and colleagues who have read drafts of one or more stories and cheered me on (with sincere apologies if I accidentally left out anyone): Debra Sue Bruck; Brenda S. Casey, RN; Amy Cherry; Margaret Deeth; Rebecca Anne Harpham; Jessica Martha Harpham; William Samuel Harpham; Pamela Jenkins, MSW; Susan Leigh, RN; Katherine H. Little, MD; David G. Maloney, MD, PhD; Diane E. Meier, MD; Adele M. O'Reilly; Joni Rodgers; Shelley Rosen; Gabriel A. Shapiro, MD; Marvin J. Stone, MD, MACP; James F. Strauss, MD; Ruth Trimmer; Benedict F. Voit; and Leonard A. Zwelling MD, MBA.

Author's Note

These stories are based on my personal experiences as a physician and a patient. To protect the privacy of others, I have changed names and altered identifying characteristics. In some cases, events have been modified and stories merged for the purpose of illustrating a point.

This book is not intended to substitute for professional care. It serves only to supplement the information provided to and by doctors, nurses, and counselors.

A Letter to Patients and Other Non-Medical Readers

Dear Patients, Family Members, Friends, and Caregivers,

I began writing these stories years ago, hoping to help healthcare professionals think and talk about compassion in modern medicine. But as the stories unexpectedly began circulating among patients, I realized they also have lessons for patients about healing.

I have included a Glossary of medical terms to give you access to the insights and information you won't find in any books or articles for lay audiences. In these pages you'll be privy to an up-close view of many of the frustrations and burdens your doctors and nurses experience while caring for patients.

This view can be healing for you, because mutual understanding paves the way to healthy relationships. So while doctors and nurses who read this book may find themselves more forgiving if a patient gets huffy or forgets an appointment, you may find yourself more accepting if your doctor doesn't thank you for a gift or doesn't say good-bye at your last visit. In addition, the stories may help you let insignificant lapses slide, thereby helping you focus on what really matters. Most importantly, you may discover ways to make it easier for your healthcare team to take good care of you. The better job they do, the better it is for you.

Because I share with clinicians many of the insights I had about myself as a patient, you may gain insight into yourself (or your loved one who is ill) as a patient. Feel free to turn around my advice for professionals and redirect it toward yourself. For example, when I say to physicians and nurses, "Remind your patients that this is not their fault. This is something we knew could happen even if everyone did everything right," you the patient can say it aloud and stop blaming yourself.

Even the most caring professionals can make a slip and unintentionally say the wrong thing. A patient once told me how her doctor said, "When things get worse ..." but because she'd read the stories, she said to herself, "My doctor really meant '*If* things get worse.'"

So use these stories to re-interpret in healing ways what your own doctors say. While you are reading *Only 10 Seconds to Care*, I hope you take comfort in knowing that today's clinicians are actively thinking and talking about how to provide compassionate care to you and all their patients.

With hope,

Wendy S. Harpham

Introduction

"Cure sometimes, relieve often, and comfort always."
Sir William Osler

Imagine a world where you leave work at the end of each shift, satisfied that you fulfilled your mission to "Cure sometimes, relieve often, and comfort always." That you provided every one of your patients with the best of modern medicine, and that you did it with patience and compassion. Impossible? It may feel so. Why?

Time. The demands on today's doctors, nurses, and allied health professionals are extraordinary. Every minute, countless tasks compete for your attention, forcing you to choose what you'll do with your limited time.

A wide variety of people can hold your patients' hands: friends, family, clergy, social workers and, nowadays, virtual support groups. But only you can provide a link to the miracles of modern medicine. At first glance, addressing your patients' feelings seems a lower priority than getting a correct diagnoses and optimizing treatments. It's not so simple.

Your relationship with your patients can mean the difference between life and death. Even if you do all the right things medically, your patients' awareness of your compassion can determine whether they report worrisome signs and symptoms in a timely manner and whether therapies are complied with. Because factors having nothing to do with the science of physical healing can affect patient outcomes, how you handle these non-medical factors may determine your success or failure in a case as well as your sense of satisfaction with your daily work.

Think about it. How do you handle patients whose fear or anger keeps them from doing what you've instructed them to do (and what you are sure they know to be the right thing)? How do you help patients who make you feel frustrated or helpless? If a patient's prognosis is grim, how can you maintain his or her hope without making false promises?

These and other questions have intrigued me since the earliest days of my medical training. From 1983 to 1990, while caring for patients in my solo practice of internal medicine at Presbyterian Hospital of Dallas, I tried to find and use healing words and actions. Listening closely to my patients' stories and reading autobiographies of patients with various diseases led me to useful insights that helped shape my everyday care of patients.

Unexpectedly in 1990, just after my 36th birthday, I was diagnosed with an indolent form of non-Hodgkins lymphoma, a slow-growing cancer with no known cure. Since then, I've been treated with radiation and intensive chemotherapy, antibody therapy in three separate clinical trials and, most recently, immunotherapy. Chronic leg pain, limited stamina, and the need for repeated courses of treatment forced me to close my medical practice in 1992 and to hang up my white coat in 1993.

It was in the setting of my own vulnerability that I first appreciated the breadth and depth of everyday difficulties endured by patients. While still in shock from the diagnosis, I found comfort in my belief that these unwanted circumstances could offer me valuable lessons about illness and healing, insights I could share with my colleagues. So just days after my diagnosis, I captured in a short essay the rush of my thoughts and feelings. My colleagues who read the final piece assured me it helped them understand.

I've been writing ever since. For the next 17 years, my readers were mostly patients, for whom I've written four guidebooks, two children's books, and innumerable articles. From the vantage of physician-survivor, I share insights and advice about treatment, recovery, long-term survivorship, raising children when a parent has cancer, and finding happiness in challenging times.

A unifying theme of all my work has been my notion of "Healthy Survivors." To understand what I mean, you need to know a little something about my experience as a patient. Just four years before my diagnosis, The National Coalition for Cancer Survivorship (NCCS) had introduced the label we now take for granted: *survivor*. Calling myself a cancer *survivor* saved me from ever feeling like a cancer *victim*.

But to put it colloquially, a survivor is "any patient who still has a pulse." "Survivor" says nothing about quality of life or the patient's role in recovery. Patients are survivors whether they are receiving excellent therapies from top-notch clinicians or they are swigging snake-oil ordered from quack Web sites. Patients in remission are survivors whether they are reveling in gratitude or are debilitated by uncontrolled fear of recurrence. As a patient, I found the term "survivor" limited.

So in 1992 I coined the term "Healthy Survivor"—a survivor who (1) gets good care and (2) lives as fully as possible. This term mobilizes patients to do the best they can do and then to accept and adjust to what is. Healthy Survivors measure success by *how* they live, not how long. Although introduced in the context of cancer survivorship, Healthy Survivors can be patients dealing with any medical challenge, from asymptomatic hypercholesterolemia to end-stage ALS.

Fairly recently, I felt compelled to return to my original audience: professionals in the healthcare system. Why? Because I know the enormous pressures you are under. Because I see the changes in medicine threatening the relationships that make our profession uniquely rewarding. And because I know more than most clinicians about how words and actions that take less than 10 seconds to say or do can change a patient's world.

With so much press and media attention focused on all that is wrong with today's healthcare, we need to start talking about all that is right and good and healing, too. I'm eager to do that because I've experienced and benefited from superb care. Like royalty, I've been cared for—and cared about—by expert clinicians who have been accessible, responsive, patient, and compassionate every step of the way. And I know good care when I see it.

Even though it has been many years since I've examined a patient or written a prescription, I've never stopped thinking like a clinician. Every year, I renew my medical license, recharging a faint hope that one day I'll be well enough to resume patient care in some form. Meanwhile, I find challenge and meaning not only in writing for patients but by serving as a sort of medical spy for healthcare professionals, relaying stories and insights from the other side of the stethoscope that may help you in your day-to-day work.

As I see it, the challenges of providing compassionate care in the modern age are inextricably linked to Healthy Survivorship. We can do our jobs better—and we can feel better about doing our jobs—by helping patients become Healthy Survivors. So the first three chapters of *Only 10 Seconds to Care* correspond to my three steps to Healthy Survivorship: Knowledge, Hope, and Action. I open the discussion by exploring how we can help our patients obtain and use sound knowledge, nourish hope, and act effectively. Because serious illness often tests faith and threatens quality of life, Chapters 4 and 5 round out the discussion by addressing how we can help patients with issues surrounding Meaning and Happiness in their lives.

I have structured the book so you can read it in brief snippets or from cover-to-cover. Each tale explores a common dilemma in patient care, focusing on how normal human emotions—both patients' and clinicians'—can get in the way of good care. Although my personal vignettes take place in the context of cancer survivorship, every story revolves around recognizing and responding to patients' unease, not disease. Thus, the stories and tips apply equally to professionals in any area of healthcare, encouraging you to reflect on your work and embrace the myriad opportunities in your busy workplace to be the compassionate clinician you set out to be.

My expectation is that for those of you—I suspect most of you—who are already doing praiseworthy jobs, reading these tales will reinforce your approach to the many challenges of patient care and help you think about compassion in practical ways. My desire is that you'll see—and seize—new opportunities for compassion that take 10 seconds or less in your everyday work. My hope is that you'll return to your patients' bedsides feeling energized and that you'll leave work at the end of the day feeling fulfilled in a whole new way.

It's time. Let's begin by exploring how to overcome problems of knowledge.

Contents

CHAPTER 1

Knowledge

"If you listen carefully to the patient they will tell you the diagnosis."

Sir William Osler

When I call my doctors because I've developed a new lump, cough, rash or other symptom, I automatically know two things: Something is wrong with me, and something will help me. My physicians and nurses use the art and science of medicine to elicit and then sift through all the clues until they arrive at the truth about my problem and the best solution.

In my medical practice, the process usually began with my taking a thorough history, a task easier said than done. Under ideal circumstances, each patient would have been a dispassionate, astute observer with sophisticated medical knowledge and a crisp memory. In real life, most of my patients were not clinicians and certainly not dispassionate. Preventing, evaluating and treating their illnesses were expensive propositions in terms of time, effort and money.

1

My office routine involved discussing with each patient how we'd work as a team at every visit—as well as between visits. I explained how we'd sleuth together, like Sherlock Holmes and Dr. Watson, for clues to the truth of the matter. I reassured them that after we knew what was wrong we'd work together in our pursuit of cures, relief and comfort. At the end of each visit, after I summarized what we knew so far, I'd teach my patient what to look for between visits and when to call or come in. It is no accident that the word "doctor" is derived from the Latin docere—to teach.

Despite my asking well-worded questions in a non-judgmental tone, vital clues occasionally remained buried. Patients' pain, desire to please, confusion or self-consciousness sometimes kept them from sharing essential bits of information. Or I blamed the time pressures and unavoidable interruptions from my staff. If not that, I pointed to the difficulty of overcoming cultural differences, patients' lack of knowledge and the wide range of patients' emotions that often got in the way of good communication.

Yet even under the best circumstances, sometimes the knowledge base my patients and I built up wasn't enough. Either the source of some of my patients' problems was destined to remain unclear until the advent of better diagnostics, or the very best available care could provide only partial relief. The most I could offer these patients was my promise to keep my eyes open for new information that might help and my reassurance that I'd hang in there with them, no matter what.

Following my first cancer surgery in 1990 and beginning the moment my eyes opened in the recovery room, a new view of knowledge slowly came into focus. I was astounded by the range and impact of medical information from non-medical sources that flooded my email inbox and curbside mailbox. I saw how my own emotions got in my way, hampering my ability to use information well. Needless to say, my understanding of knowledge—how patients obtain, process and share information—has evolved since my white coat days as a young, healthy clinician.

In this chapter, I share stories of my struggles regarding knowledge. My encouraging you to think about the context in which your patients hear what you tell them may help everyone—you, your patients and their caregivers—better understand why patients might question indisputable facts about treatment options or consider kooky theories about the causes of their illnesses. You'll read the insights that rejuvenated my patience when taking a history felt like pulling teeth and find tips about helping patients do a better job. You'll be encouraged to think about why patients might lie—by omission or overtly, and to consider ways you can help patients share painful truths. You'll discover of why sometimes your patients want you to tell them what to do and why at other times they want to be the one commanding their course of treatment.

The Internet and the patient empowerment movement have changed the landscape of clinician-patient relationships in dramatic ways, impacting how patients deal with uncertainty about their diagnoses and prognoses. You'll read about times when the right answer is the wrong answer, and when there are no answers at all.

The stethoscope helps you hear your patient's heart sounds; understanding helps you know and touch your patient's heart. With knowledge of the facts being the first step to understanding, knowledge is power. Nowhere is this truer than in the world of medicine.

I Can't Remember

In medical school, we are taught the key to a timely, correct diagnosis is taking a thorough, accurate medical history. Yet when we try to speed things up in our offices, the history-taking often becomes one of the most frustrating aspects of our day. In the interest of knowledge, we can take steps to help patients provide useful histories.

"When did your pain begin?" Such a simple question. You'd think if people are hurting, they'd know when their pain began. But this patient hesitates, unable to decide if it was two weeks earlier or four. "I can't remember."

She reminds me of a painful admission from my internship year: a middle-aged patient who was transferred to our hospital at the end of my long night on call. The patient was weary but alert. She knew nothing about why she was transferred or what her treatments had been, so I turned my attention to her current symptoms. When I asked about her pain, she looked blankly at me, "I can't remember."

My patience started to slip, tugged by sleep deprivation and the paper in my pocket listing test results to check and people to see before morning rounds began in an hour. This patient wasn't helping. So I took a breath and curled my toes, and counted to three, and rubbed my nose to keep from showing my frustration.

Later that day, I learned my effort had failed. The attending physician towered over me, telling me in no uncertain terms that healers do not make patients feel bad when they can't give a crisp history. My moment of shame stayed with me for years, fortifying my patience whenever I cared for poor historians. This calm didn't keep me from wondering how patients could be so bad at a task so important and seemingly easy.

My belief in the power of a good history was reinforced by my own diagnosis. Throughout my first courses of cancer treatments, I could rattle off my history like a well-prepared intern presenting to the chief of medicine. I was determined to make my doctors' job as easy as possible, so they could do their best to help me. The challenge for me wasn't giving a history, but rather learning how to live well between office visits.

Distraction paved my road to happiness. I got really good at focusing on non-illness-related tasks, creating so-called flow that has freed me from my chronic neuropathic leg pain as effectively as analgesics. Now when I leave for the chemo-room, my laptop and manuscripts tucked snugly in my backpack, I tell myself "I'm going to Suite 700 to work on Chapter 9. And yeah, sure, while I'm there I'll roll up my sleeve and get some cancer treatment, too." Should I find it hard to focus on writing, I'm equipped to fool myself into having fun with comic books, music CDs and snacks. You see, if I don't pay attention to the IVs and medicine-y smell, I don't store memories of the missed needlesticks and my nausea.

Over time, the repeated courses of treatment have taken their toll on my short-term memory and everyday stamina. It's become easier and easier to ignore and forget, and not just because—to put it bluntly—I am less sharp and more tired. Some of my deficit has been learned. As a patient living in the well world, choosing to ignore my tolerable discomforts and forget about my cancer helps me enjoy the life I have.

Dates of upcoming scans and checkups no longer serve as indelible reference points in time, unlike during the first years of my illness. Would you believe I now leave sticky notes on my bathroom mirror so I don't forget to fast and go? The first time I almost missed an appointment, I celebrated: "See? Cancer is not the center of my life!" I am happier with my illness hazy in the periphery of my thoughts, as long as—and only if—I am doing the right things medically to get better.

Patients' cloudy minds are a problem, of course, when worrisome symptoms arise or treatable conditions persist. Physicians depend on their patients to be their eyes and ears between office visits. That transfer patient from years ago who couldn't give the lowly intern—me—her history was not at risk, because her attending knew her story well. But patients who are poor historians pay a steep price if their forgotten details are the keys to getting good care.

Patients need our understanding and support. In the spirit of teamwork, patients can be taught tricks, such as "Keep a symptom diary," and can be given prompts, such as "Was it before or after…(your birthday, whatever holiday, your trip to wherever)?" If patients' cognitive deficits, depression, fatigue, or adaptive repression make giving a history too difficult, their family and friends must become their eyes and ears and voice.

I was really scared the day I answered my oncologist, "I can't remember." Not only because of the new pain that signaled another recurrence, but because I honestly didn't know if my pain had begun two weeks earlier or four. Committed to both getting good care and living fully, I stopped on my way home from my doctor's office and bought myself a crutch: a spiral notebook. Why? Because I'll keep ignoring and forgetting, partly because my brain doesn't work as well and partly because between office visits I am happier when I do. However hard it gets, my doctors and I will find ways to deal with it. "I can't remember" is a problem to be solved, not my destiny.

- We help patients remember important details by cueing them with references to milestones and holidays and by suggesting they keep symptom diaries.
- We protect patients' dignity by acknowledging the benefit of downplaying their discomforts between office visits and then emphasizing, "but only if doing so doesn't impede good care."
- We help relieve patients' burden by encouraging family and friends to assist with the history, when needed.

Secrets and Lies

It's one thing if our patients struggle to provide an accurate history. It's quite another if our patients are deliberately leaving out critical details or lying. The facts of a case have to be true to be useful. So we have to find ways to help patients overcome the obstacles to telling the whole truth.

"Do patients ever keep secrets from their physicians? Do they ever lie?"

These are just two of many questions I'm preparing for a guest lecture to an undergraduate ethics class. While most academic discussions focus on physicians' professional obligation to maintain confidentiality (except when life or limb is at stake), I want this class to explore the patient dynamics.

I've lumped together secrets and lies because the fundamental problem is the same: For whatever reason, patients keep some fact(s) to themselves or distort a truth.

As a medical student, I was introduced to secrets and lies as obstacles to ideal patient care. My mentors taught me how patients' past experiences and beliefs can affect what patients say. These professors kept hammering into me that the key to proper diagnoses and treatments is taking a thorough and accurate history. So I strove to perfect my delivery of open-ended, non-judgmental questions and thus facilitate wide-open communication.

By the time I hung my shiny new shingle outside Suite 508, I was adept at using the same tone of voice whether asking patients "How many cups of coffee and/or tea do you drink daily?" or "How many men and/or women do you sleep with?" I asked patients the names of all the prescription, over-the-counter, alternative and illicit drugs they used. I provided spaces to record the number of spontaneous and therapeutic abortions as well as live- and stillbirths.

Normalizing sensitive information paved the way for full disclosure. Or so I naively thought. One day a chart with the results of a new patient's screening blood work was placed on my desk. The delightful octogenarian I'd met the day before had a positive VDRL. Only after her old records finally arrived did I learn she'd already been adequately treated for both latent and neurosyphilis. Twice.

After telling the students this anecdote and describing my shock, I might recite a cynical aphorism from internship days: "Whatever patients say, multiply the number of cigarettes by two and ounces of alcohol by four." Then I can jump-start the class discussion with a provocative question: "Won't pervasive skepticism risk destroying the mutual trust necessary for optimal care?"

Since effective solutions begin with understanding the problems, I'll prompt the students: "Why might patients lie?" After they volunteer ideas, I can share stories about patients who lie to keep up the "good patient" image or to escape being admonished for not complying with physical therapy or a low-salt diet. Or about patients who falsely deny having a seizure, so their doctors won't take away their car keys again. And sadly, about patients who insist they are doing fine, covering up their misery from the side effects of salvage therapies out of fear their doctors will give up on them.

If the ethics class needs some zing, I can relate my own stupid blunder. For idiotic reasons that somehow made sense to me in the hurricane of first-remission emotions, I chose to take a medication incorrectly, instead of discussing my concerns with my physician. When a new symptom popped up, I felt obligated to confess. I can paint a picture for the students of how my face flushed with embarrassment and shame, feelings that lingered for years.

Under certain circumstances and for a variety of reasons, patients can be afraid to tell the truth. Some patients practice their deception for days, while others are surprised by a response that escapes their lips at a doctor visit. Whether deliberate or subconscious, these deceptions reflect patients' fear of the truth that overwhelms their desire to help their situation by providing an accurate history—even if only momentarily.

Note that sometimes patients' fears have nothing whatsoever to do with their physicians. Talking about a particular topic to *anyone* stirs patients' painful feelings of embarrassment or shame, or regret-filled distress about past choices. So even when patients want their physicians in on their secret and trust their physicians to react with gracious understanding, they still may clam up out of fear they'll be asked about it or offered sympathy, either of which they couldn't handle now.

What's a clinician to do? For starters, when you suspect something might be awry, invite patients to share any secrets or something they said "that may have come out wrong." Help patients save face by offering something like, "Lapses happen. Patients are just trying to make things work out okay when they are afraid to tell the truth."

Then you can help them overcome their fear by focusing on the shared mission. "I need to know everything—the good and the bad, the silly and the embarrassing—to do all I can to take good care of you." And since friends sometimes keep secrets to prevent hurt feelings or other problems, acknowledging and then moving away from any such camaraderie may help, too: "We've become friends over the years, and this is great. But when dealing with medical issues, our relationship has to be professional, not social."

Patients may relax if they know you won't scold or pry. "You said you drink three beers a day. If the number is really six, I just need to know that to help me make the right diagnoses and prescribe the right treatments. We don't have to talk about your drinking."

Secrets and lies are more than problems to solve. They are opportunities for healing.

In some cases, a clinician's quiet listening to a painful secret is the best cure of all. Physicians who respond without anger, frustration or disappointment spare their patients from additional feelings of vulnerability and loss of control, feelings that may have prompted the lies in the first place.

Whatever the case, the truth can set patients and their physicians free. Together, physicians and patients can move forward toward the best possible solutions.

- Patients' deceptions reflect their fear of telling the truth, a feeling that overwhelms their desire to provide the most useful history.
- We can help patients save face by saying something like, "Lapses happen."
- Patients may share unpleasant truths if reassured we won't scold or pry.

Misunderstanding Physicians

We grow up learning to say, "I understand" after someone shares complicated or emotionally charged information. This expression of empathy encourages people to continue providing information and reassures them that their information is safe with us. Unfortunately, in clinical settings this everyday phrase can cause trouble.

Pauline's lower lip starts to quiver while telling our support group about her most recent checkup. She then turns to me, "After I confided how scared I was, my oncologist gently put his hand on mine. Nodding sympathetically, he said to me, 'I understand.'"

In the momentary silence, during which Pauline takes a breath, my mind flashes to similar scenes from my practice. I remember the effort it took to block out everything else from my mind while listening to my patients. Now and then, I would repeat the gist of what they had just said, so they could confirm I'd gotten the message right.

My fleeting reverie is disrupted by Pauline's out-burst, "Understand? No way! He's great—I love him as my doctor—but…"

I've never seen Pauline like this, wagging her index finger at me as she continues her rant, "No, ma'am. Don't try to tell me he *understands*."

How could Pauline feel angry after describing a doctor who appreciated her distress and responded with sympathy?

Maybe Pauline sensed an attempt to shut down the emotionally charged line of discussion with a self-serving platitude. But I doubt it. More likely, the problem stems from a common mistake, one with which I'm familiar as both a physician and a patient.

Before my diagnosis, I read autobiographies of people with various diseases and injuries. In my office, hoping to better understand the illness experience, I paid attention to the details of my patients' stories. On occasion while driving home, I projected what it would be like if it were me.

Yet years later, when possibility became reality and I was diagnosed with cancer, I was shocked by how shocked I was. That first week, one phrase about serious illness kept replaying over and over in my head: "I didn't have a clue." Reflecting on past conversations where I had felt tuned in to my patients, I now thought, "I never really understood."

What does it mean for a doctor to "understand"?

Flipping the components of this compound word—stand under—paints a lovely image: positioning you lower than someone else, so that the knowledge or emotions of another can flow into you. But real-life communicating is rarely that easy.

Messages can get garbled, even when both parties make every effort to be clear. As Robert McClosky, the 20th century American author, once said, "I know that you believe you understand what you think I said, but I'm not sure you realize that what you heard is not what I meant."

To complicate matters, "understanding" is not one distinct process. Understanding why water expands when frozen presents a different challenge than understanding another person's emotions.

Dealing with patients' emotions is a vital task for healthcare professionals. Unfortunately, it's too easy for patients and their doctors to jumble different types of understanding. This confusion cuts to the heart of the problem that causes some patients to bristle in response to "I understand."

When physicians speak as professionals, "I understand" means "I detect your fear, sadness, or confusion." It means "I have expertise regarding the causes and consequences of these emotions, as well as healing interventions." This intellectual type of understanding reassures patients who worry that they are abnormal in some way—weak, overly dramatic, or even crazy—or that nothing can be done.

Since medicine will always be, at its core, people caring for people, "I understand" also means, "I, too, have experienced dangers in my life and am familiar with the distress caused by unpleasant emotions." In contrast to the intellectual type of understanding, this type is based on empathy.

But Pauline's anger suggests that her physician's expertise and caring were not enough. She felt that short of walking in the same shoes her physician could never quite understand. This brings to mind a time I was struggling with interferon-related fatigue, a frustrating and demoralizing exhaustion unlike any I'd ever experienced. One day I met another survivor who said, "Wendy, I know exactly what you mean. I'm on interferon, too, and I'm whipped." An indescribable relief washed over me with the realization, "Ah, someone who *really* understands."

This third type of understanding—what some might consider a deeper form of empathic understanding—is uniquely healing, which explains why support groups work well for many patients.

The crux of the problem is that with so many different definitions, "I understand" can be heard one way when intended another way. Some patients yearn—even if only subconsciously—for connection with someone who has been similarly sick. Through no fault of their physicians or nurses, such patients might feel put off or, worse, alienated from the healthcare team if told, "I understand."

Until we develop a vocabulary that accounts for the nuances of the various types of understanding, physicians and nurses can acknowledge the divide while reaching across with expertise and caring. As my oncologist said after diagnosing my first recurrence, "I can only imagine what this feels like, but I'll do all I can to help you."

When we assure patients that we understand, let's make sure we do understand.

> - Acknowledging an inability to know what it's like can be more healing than inferring complete understanding.
> - We reassure patients by telling them we don't need to have experienced the same illness to help them deal with their illness.
> - We encourage healing by reaching out with expertise, advice and comfort.

Square Pegs

Practicing medicine is never boring because every patient is like a puzzle. In order to exchange the information that enables us to solve the puzzle of his or her illness, we first must solve the puzzle of each patient's communication style and needs. Labeling patients provides a shortcut, but at the risk of leading us astray.

As a kindergartner clutching a square peg, I learned to avoid frustration by skipping the round spaces and only trying the square holes. This lesson served me well for decades after graduating from the block station.

In my medical office, pegging patients improved the flow. Structured questions reined in my patients who tended to ramble. Frequent prompts encouraged my stoics through the storytelling half of the "H & P." By routinely allotting more time for my information junkies, I didn't get (too) far behind schedule.

More importantly, cataloguing patients enhanced the healing. Even something as simple as finishing one patient's visit with a firm handshake and another's with a gentle hug helped to reinforce these patients' self-confidence and their trust in me.

When interns were assigned to my service, I encouraged them to pay attention to each patient's style. We discussed how a patient's needs could almost be predicted by considering their cultural background, education, and personality and, of course, the patient's past coping style.

The interns marveled at self-educated patients who mastered the ins-and-outs of their illnesses. These patients often dismissed authoritarian doctors, preferring physicians who assumed the role of advisor or even quasi-employee.

I warned the newly minted doctors to be prepared for patients who couldn't handle any medical information or decision-making. Lopsided in the extreme, these relationships worked best when the clinician revived the paternalistic doctor of yesteryear.

Looking back, I don't see anything really wrong with what I taught the interns. But after years of living on the patient side of the stethoscope, I realize that my message missed its mark. The notion of matching my professional approach to the needs of the particular patient was on-target. Labeling patients was where I fell short.

To illustrate, I'll tell you about three patients whom I came to know well while I was being treated. They all were under the care of the same physician, but these patients were as different from each other as chocolate, vanilla and strawberry.

The first patient was post-op and on morphine. Two days earlier, she'd learned she had cancer. Suspended in la-la land—still reeling from the shock and recovering from surgery—she was well-served by her oncologist when he presented her chemo regimen as a prescription at the time of discharge, much the way I'd prescribe antibiotics for a patient's pneumonia.

The second patient sat on the edge of her seat in her oncologist's office, not looking or acting the least bit sick. Like a grandmother whipping out a wallet-full of baby photos, the patient opened a manila folder filled with newspaper clippings and highlighted reprints of medical articles.

A fly on the wall might easily have mistaken them for two consulting physicians, the way she rattled off in medical lingo the advantages and disadvantages of each treatment option and expounded on theories behind various investigational therapies. But the gig would be up when the patient ended her monologue, "This treatment seems best, but what do *you* recommend?"

As for the last patient, anyone would have realized she was distressed during her consultation. As the patient later recounted, "I pinched the bridge of my nose to keep from crying. My oncologist handed me a box of tissues and leaned back, giving me time to gather myself." She paused for effect and then continued with a twinkle, "I dabbed my eyes and, between that crazy mixture of crying and laughing, told him, 'You can keep talking. I'm not a blithering idiot; I'm just blithering.'"

Looking back at these patients, the surprise is not that the oncologist deftly matched his style to each of them, but that these three dramatically different patients were, in fact, one and the same person—me.

Four days before my diagnosis I was training for recertification in advanced cardiac life support. Yet when a decision needed to be made about how to save my life, I was useless. My oncologist and internist properly judged that I was totally incapable of critical thinking, and they didn't even try to involve me.

Many recurrences later, living with lymphoma was my "new normal." When decisions had to be made, I could easily dissociate from myself and become, in effect, an impartial spectator. My physicians welcomed my input whenever I chose to bring my clinical acumen to the decision-making regarding my own care.

Perhaps most interesting was that time I couldn't keep from crying in my oncologist's office. After my oncologist reviewed all my options, he asked, "Wendy, what treatment do *you* want to do?"

Feeling physically sick and emotionally worn out, I told him, "I understand everything, but, please, just tell me what to do."

My oncologist never knows exactly which Wendy he's going to see when I show up. Depending on how well I'm feeling, how dire the prognosis and how difficult the choices, I can be any one of a wide variety of patient "types."

When doing a children's puzzle, square pegs are always square. But patients are not blocks of wood, and risk lies in assuming a square peg is always square.

When caring for patients, the challenge is helping them heal no matter what shape they are in.

- Tailoring care to the needs of each patient improves both the communication and the potential for healing.
- Patients' needs and coping styles may shift dramatically from time to time, depending on how well they feel, how dire the prognoses, how difficult the choices, and a host of other factors.
- Labeling patients increases the risk of mismatching our approach to their current needs.

Only a Click Away

Sophisticated technology has changed how patients obtain information, as well as how we diagnose disease and follow patients' responses to therapy. Problems can arise when patients search the Internet for medical information. Problems also can arise if we forget about the effects of radiological studies on our patients.

The importance of weighing risks and benefits before writing a prescription can't be overstated: First do no harm. But a recent episode reminds me this aphorism does not just refer to treatments.

I'm walking briskly toward a store with my to-do list in my hand, when I realize I might not have locked my car. So I turn around and walk back toward my minivan, clicking my keyless remote every two steps while listening for the *honk* that acknowledges activation of the locking mechanism.

A man hops out of his pickup truck and crosses over to me. "This is going to sound wacko," he says, "but if you put your remote in your mouth, the signal reaches much farther."

"For real?" I ask. He nods. I thank him, and we go our separate ways.

After completing my errand, I head back toward my car. And yes, I put the key fob in my mouth as I click it. Sure enough, the car unlocks from an impressive distance. At home, I don't bother to look up why the remote trick might work or even if it's a real phenomenon. All I know is that it seems to be true.

A week later, I attend a meeting downtown. Two hours later, tired and hungry, I go straight to where I remember parking my car. My minivan isn't there! So I walk around the underground lot with my keyless remote in my mouth, pressing the panic button, hoping to target my car by sounding its horn. No such luck.

At first I wonder if the mouth trick only works for the locking mechanism, but that doesn't make much sense. So I keep walking and clicking, 'round and 'round to the same spot on each level of the lot where I thought I parked my car. Suddenly it hits me: I borrowed my son's car. My minivan is at home, 15 miles away.

I am so amused by my "clicker episode" that I post about it on my blog, hoping the vignette will provide balance to my soapbox soliloquies on the importance of obtaining sound knowledge. Maybe I can prevent some survivors from becoming consumed or paralyzed by a perceived need to research every sneeze, concluding that: Every decision doesn't have to be a major chore. Does it?"

Within an hour—*bing*—a comment pops up on my blog. "Wendy, such an interesting phenomena has to have been researched," writes Debby. She includes hyperlinks to sites that explain the physics behind the amplified remote signal, including a link to a video. Seconds later, I'm watching a man putting his remote under his chin.

"Great. A less dorky-looking way to increase my remote's range," I think, now wishing I had a way to contact the man in the pickup.

That the phenomenon can be explained by science is no surprise. What takes away my breath is realizing all over again how easily people can access reader-friendly explanations. Learning almost anything is only a click away. The challenge for patients—and their healthcare teams—becomes ensuring that all the garbage information is sifted out.

I read the end of Debby's message, and my stomach sinks. "My only concern is shooting beams of energy into the head. Don't know if there are any studies done on side effects from doing that."

I can't believe I published a blog post that condones taking action without first obtaining sound knowledge.

Bing—Debby posts another comment, complete with more URLs. "Studies today have shown links between cell phones and brain cancer."

A new wave of queasiness washes over me. I'm not worried that my recent clicking in my mouth has increased my risk of brain cancer. No, I feel sick because I let down my guard.

Like me with my clicker-in-the-mouth, physicians have been embracing new diagnostic technologies. When a patient presents with a suspicious pain or lump, few responses can clarify the situation as quickly and definitively as ordering a scan. But what's the risk?

I remember being seized by fear when my oncologist ordered another CT with contrast to evaluate my second recurrence in 1993. The caring radiologist tried to reassure me about the radiation risk: "Wendy, this scan is a drop in the bucket compared to the rads you received with your mini-mantle last summer."

For a fleeting moment, I imagined a bulging meniscus atop a bucket of water, and the scan I was about to undergo being the "drop" that caused carcinogenic mutations in the DNA of my healthy cells. But with the immediate threat of my lymphoma overwhelmingly outweighing the distant threat of a second malignancy, I submitted willingly to the scan.

Eighteen years and five bulging x-ray jackets after my diagnosis, additional x-ray exposure is no small matter for me. My oncologist agrees, weighing the risks and benefits of each diagnostic test as carefully as he weighs each treatment option before writing any prescriptions. When he is sure it won't compromise my evaluation, he orders alternative imaging methods. And he orders screening x-rays and CT scans only when the benefit clearly outweighs the risk, hoping to avoid my tipping point for inducing a second malignancy.

First do no harm. Until scientists clarify the risk, I'm holding my keyless remote as far from my head as possible, even when this means walking a few extra steps. Besides, the exercise does me good.

- We help patients obtain knowledge by addressing information they obtain from the Internet and by guiding patients to reputable resources.
- We help patients make wise decisions by weighing the risks and benefits of each diagnostic test as carefully as we weigh each treatment option.
- We help patients heal by listening to and acknowledging expressed fears of diagnostic tests and helping them put the risks of tests in perspective.

Informed Consent

I was good at getting my patients to sign informed consent forms. Or at least I thought I was until I had to sign such a form before participating in a clinical trial.

One essential chore stands between the patient and the physician's knife or catheter: obtaining informed consent. Physicians and nurses are obligated to get each patient's John Hancock to make the permission official.

As an internist, the only interventions done in my office that required a release form were sigmoidoscopies. Informed consent served as my legal safety net by documenting that my patients were both knowledgeable and free in their decision to proceed.

With triplicate forms in hand, I carefully modulated the tone of my voice, striving to communicate the threats without scaring my patients out of signing. Obviously I'd already recommended the procedure to my prepped-and-gowned patients. Invariably I'd also shared my confidence that the benefits outweighed the risks.

If patients hesitated, I assured them I was familiar with and prepared to address potential complications. I often repeated how I'd seen the desired outcome often enough to expect the same for them. That I never had a patient balk at the dotted line suggested a job well done. Yet in the spring of '93, I discovered a better way.

I was a cancer patient facing my second recurrence and frightened beyond words. I forced myself to shift into disciplined-doctor mode, knowing that wise treatment decisions must be made dispassionately. Wishes and hopes must be shoved aside, just for the moment, while statistics reign supreme.

Taking notes helped me make sense of my telephone consultations with various experts around the country. To sum up what I'd learned, I designed a crude chart that weighed the advantages and disadvantages of my best options. (Interestingly, physicians who do this for their patients are called "admirably thorough," while patients who do this for themselves might easily be labeled "obsessive-compulsive.")

A week's worth of serious talks and salty tears later, my husband and I met with my local oncologist to make a final decision. We reviewed the options again and unanimously agreed I should enroll in one particular trial.

So my husband and I made arrangements. A few days later, we flew out west to meet the research team. After doing a history and physical, the same researcher from my earlier phone calls once again discussed my options, as well as the risks and benefits of the trial. Then we were ushered into a conference room to fill out the informed consent forms for the following day's treatment.

Weak and worn out, both physically and emotionally, I experienced a bizarre disequilibrium as I entered the room. The research nurse started reading the form aloud, pointing to each potential complication. Knowing that once treated I could never go back and undo what had been done, I urged myself, "Pay attention, Wendy." Lord knows I tried, following the tip of her finger as if it were the bouncing ball over the words to a sing-along. But the words looked and sounded like gibberish.

Nothing would have been lost had the nurse thumbed quickly through the pages to the signature line at the end, the way I now scroll down quickly to the "I accept" box whenever signing up for Internet access in a hotel. I had let go of my objectivity the moment I left my local oncologist's office to purchase plane tickets for the trial.

With the nurse's pen in my hand and my survival instincts in full gear, I tuned out her recitation of potential complications. I could no more have refused consent than I could have made an about-face at the altar and left my wedding without saying, "I do." For me, this mind-numbing formality simply legalized the many meaningful conversations that had led up to my commitment to the trial. And that was okay.

Wait! We're talking about my signing a legal document regarding life-and-death treatment.

Yes, but as a patient about to undergo an investigational therapy, I couldn't focus on all that could go wrong, even for a few moments. Doing so would have made it far more difficult to psych myself up for the imminent treatment. Letting go of my objectivity was more than okay; it was exactly what I needed to do.

I'm sure I'm not the only patient who zones out when presented with a consent form. So what are clinicians to do?

It makes sense to include obtaining informed consent with the other pre-treatment preparations. This ensures the signed forms get into patients' charts. But this timing can create problems for patients: The mindset necessary for giving informed consent is distinctly "un-healing" for patients about to undergo treatment.

Maybe hospitals and medical practices could first present consent forms when patients are still in critical-thinking mode, such as immediately following the treatment decision. This would lend itself to careful patient review and opportunities for the healthcare team to address their questions. Signatures would signify thoughtful consent.

Later, when patients are eventually admitted to the clinic or hospital for treatment, they could be handed their consent forms once again. Only this time the expectation would be for patients to flip right to the signature line, where the addition of their initials would confirm they hadn't changed their mind. Certainly, patients who wanted to review all the details yet again could be encouraged to do so.

Clinicians know that informed consent is a process, not a piece of paper. A two-stage signing might help the consent form function as intended: to promote patients' clear understanding. Getting the "informed" part of the consent completed early, patients can then approach treatment with a healing blend of optimism and hope. With the frightening facts no longer forced in front of them, patients may do better medically. For sure, they'll feel better.

- Informed consent is a process, not a piece of paper.
- The mindset necessary for giving informed consent is distinctly un-healing for patients about to undergo a procedure or treatment.
- We can offer patients a two-stage signing process: Immediately following the decision-making process, they can sign the consent form. Later, just before proceeding with the procedure or treatment, they can initial their signature.

My Bed Buddy and Me

Despite our best efforts to explain what we know—and what we don't know—about why things are the way they are, our patients can come up with the most interesting explanations. In addition to sharing the known facts about our patients' illnesses, we can clarify any misinformation that is burdening patients with diseases or complications that are not at all their fault.

The news was bad: My lymphoma was back. Again. My first thought? "My Bed Buddy. I've recurred because I've been sleeping with my new Bed Buddy."

Who's this sleep-mate? For those who know I'm happily married, no need to worry. Bed Buddy is a blue sock filled with rice. On cold winter nights, after three minutes in the microwave, my Bed Buddy keeps my toes toasty until long after I fall asleep. A few months before that cancer recurrence, my husband, Ted, had found the perfect gift for me. Well, perfect until Bed Buddy stirred up the quiescent cancer cells.

What?! Did I really believe a rice-filled sock caused cancer? No, of course not. But truth be told, the absurd thought did cross my mind, causing me to laugh aloud and then dismiss it two seconds later. What's going on? Why would I blame Bed Buddy, even for a second? I think I know.

As a physician, I cared for patients like Bonnie and Jimmy, salt-of-the earth hardworking people struggling with diseases I'd hoped and prayed I'd never get. My Bonnies and Jimmys taught me bad things can happen for no good reason. And during all those years of practicing internal medicine, I was well-aware that my white coat did not protect me in some magical way.

Which is why when my oncologist gently broke the news of my lymphoma all I could think was, "Why *not* me?" The idea that cancer was punishment for something I'd done wrong seemed as ridiculous as the belief that Santa Claus recorded when I was naughty or nice.

Granted, in the weeks following my original diagnosis, I did look for a reason for my cancer. Friends and family kept asking me: "What were you exposed to?" or "Could it be from the nearby power lines?" I called my oncologist when our elderly black lab was found to have enlarged lymph nodes. I called him again after learning that four of my high school classmates had been treated for various types of lymphoma. Finding a reason for my cancer wouldn't change that I was sick, but it helped keep the world from seeming totally senseless. More importantly, understanding might provide a way I could protect my children.

Many of the proposed culprits suggested by family and friends were acquitted by sound scientific studies. As for the few known risk factors for my type of lymphoma, I had none. My faith comforted me, a strong belief that persistent researchers would eventually determine the specific events that caused 14-18 chromosomal translocations (such as those in my cancer cells) and then use this knowledge to find ways to prevent this type of lymphoma. But my persistent speculation about the cause of my lymphoma was not healing; I had to let go of the blame-game and move forward.

My being a physician helped me accept that I could *affect,* but *not control,* the outcome. I'd seen too many Bonnies and Jimmys do everything right and still die.

Yet for a short while after my first recurrence—longer than I'd like to admit—I was troubled by a disquieting sense of guilt and responsibility. For this, I blame friends' insensitive comments such as, "Maybe your cancer recurred because you went back to work too soon," or others' urgings, "You should eat more vegetables, exercise less, do yoga, and take this supplement." Unwittingly, in their efforts to empower me they were blaming me and making my life harder.

Despite great confidence in my approach to healing and my team of superb physicians and nurses, the unsolicited advice was hard to dismiss without a twinge of hesitation. After all, if someone could point out something I was doing wrong, then I could fix it and get well.

In the universal human quest for control, we are wired to connect the dots. We search obsessively and often unconsciously for cause and effect. This trait is adaptive, helping protect us from eating poisonous berries or touching a hot stove a second time. But observation and instinct can fool us. So as we grow up, science helps us to distinguish true cause-and-effect relationships from those that are illusions. This knowledge enables us, both as individuals and as a species, to acquire more and more control over our environment and our fate. It also frees us from beliefs that are a waste of time and energy or, worse, may lead us to disaster.

When faced with terrible illness that is nobody's fault, patients often look for someone or something to blame. And too many times, often without even realizing it, they are blaming themselves. That day I learned my cancer had recurred, I wasn't just blaming my Bed Buddy. I was blaming myself for wanting warm toes, for using Bed Buddy, and for this terrible thing that was happening to me.

Clinicians help patients who are diagnosed with complications or disease flares that are beyond anyone's control by taking a few seconds to emphasize, "This is not your fault. This is something we knew could happen even if everyone did everything right. Let's see what we can do now to help." Sometimes bad things happen. Let's not blame Bed Buddy.

- We can acknowledge the natural human tendency to attribute cause-and-effect when two things happen together, as well as patients' natural desire to search for causes of their illnesses even when nobody is to blame.
- We can warn patients of loved ones' tendency to lay blame, even if unintentional.
- We help patients heal by stating definitively when misfortune is not their fault.

A Certain Uncertainty

The best you can do is the best you can do. But sometimes patients want more: They want to be cured. While using the science and art of medicine to minimize the uncertainty regarding a patient's health, we can help patients accept a certain uncertainty.

Marveling at my remission, Jane asks, "Wendy, don't you wish you *knew* if you were cured?"

"NO!" I respond immediately.

"No?" My friend sounds shocked.

Actually my answer makes perfect sense, since there are only two ways to know if my cancer is gone for good. If the lymphoma recurs, I'll know I wasn't cured. If my cancer is in remission when I die of something else, I'll know I was.

Many years ago, after my first course of chemotherapy, I considered "cure" the capstone of survivorship. With cure's aura of freedom from the uncertainties of illness, no other outcome could better help me move on.

As healthcare professionals, we deal with uncertainty all the time. In our hospitals and offices, we strive to minimize ambiguity. I definitely feel better saying, "Ms. Smith, I can assure you with 95% certainty that…" rather than saying, "Ms. Smith, I can only tell you with 25% certainty that…"

When caring for patients who are reluctant to proceed with tests and procedures, it's a common practice for us to encourage them by dangling the carrot of certainty: "This loads-of-fun whatever-oscopy will help us know *for sure* what's causing your problem."

Whether our evaluation nails down our patient's exact diagnosis or determines only what our patient certainly does *not* have, our prescription-writing is, at best, a sophisticated game of trial-and-error. If the evidence-based first-choice treatment doesn't work or causes intolerable side effects, we switch to a second-line treatment, and so on. Uncertainty is part and parcel of practicing medicine.

Many of us feel anxious when we aren't sure of the diagnosis or best therapy. Ideally, this adaptive discomfort prompts us to reexamine our patient's case more closely or to consult with a colleague. Once reassured we are doing our best, our composure returns along with our acceptance that diagnoses occasionally remain unclear, and unexpected or unwanted outcomes happen.

My experience as a physician with such uncertainty shaped my early survivorship. I welcomed the surgeries, blood tests and scans that helped my oncologist accurately diagnose and stage my disease. During the months of chemotherapy, I gladly adjusted my schedule whenever my oncologist delayed a dose, knowing he was walking the fine line between under- and over-treating me.

Satisfying my intellectual desire for certainty by taking steps that optimized my recovery helped me get good care. But it did surprisingly little to calm the anxiety triggered by not knowing what was happening in my body between visits and what my next scans would show. I needed something in addition to the favorable statistical probabilities.

First, I tried expecting the worst, and it made me depressed. Then I tried expecting the best, but the effort of denying unpleasant possibilities was exhausting. So I tried expecting both the worst and the best at the same time, and it just about made me crazy.

The hospital oncology social worker suggested I join a support group to explore techniques for calming the fear of recurrence.

In response, I teased, "Or I could buy myself a CT scanner and do a self-exam every morning. Whadya-think?"

Poker-faced, she responded, "If you think you need a normal CT scan to enjoy your day, aren't you suggesting that everybody needs a daily scan?"

Her message was clear: Illness doesn't make life uncertain; illness simply exposes the uncertainty of life. She was right, of course.

So I joined a support group where I could learn from veteran survivors how to embrace life after cancer. I was still on the steep slope of the learning curve when my cancer came back.

Using typical Harpham sick humor to soften my news, I announced to my support group pals in a borscht-belt New York accent, "I found the cure for fear of recurrence: Go ahead and have one. Then you'll stop worrying about it!"

While everyone laughed, it hit me: In some situations, certainty comes at too terrible a price.

After cancer, uncertainty can create anxiety that steals survivors' joy. As healthcare professionals, we help our patients by reassuring them that we are doing all we can to minimize the uncertainty associated with their diagnoses and treatments. And we help them by emphasizing the difference between this statistical uncertainty and the uncertainty of survivorship, which is simply the universal uncertainty of life, up close and personal. For those patients who might be struggling, we can refer them to resources equipped to guide and support them in their personal quests for calm.

Nowadays—most of the time, anyway—I'm too focused on what's happening today to worry about tomorrow. All my writing and talking and laughing and crying helped me find ways to live well with the uncertainty. That's why, as I told my befuddled friend, when I am in remission and my future is anyone's guess, I really don't want to know if I am cured.

When it comes to living well after cancer, a certain uncertainty is a wonderful thing.

- When no curative treatments are available, we can acknowledge patients' desire for cure while guiding them toward goals that are within reach.
- We help patients deal with uncertainty by explaining how we use knowledge about populations to care for individuals.
- We can reassure patients regarding things we can guarantee: doing our best every day while looking for medical advances that might help.

Puzzling

As clinicians, we are trained to think "horses," not "zebras" when we hear hoof beats. So it can be quite a problem when a patient's constellation of symptoms or medical course doesn't fit any known diagnosis or pattern. A big problem. And not just for us.

All the experts—infectious disease, allergy, cardiology, even my usually unstumpable chief of internal medicine—were puzzled by Rita Sue. Timely resuscitation had saved her, but nobody had a clue what had caused her thready pulse and undetectable blood pressure. Curbside conversations hadn't been that animated about something other than Medicare reimbursement in years. The buzz was energizing, but the fact that our mystery was linked to Rita Sue's misery disturbed me.

Most healthcare professionals I know like challenges. Patients' symptoms prompt our puzzle-solving evaluations and prescriptions. We feel the heady power of medical knowledge when what is frightening or confusing for our patients is ho-hum for us. Walking the well-worn steps of treatment algorithms fills our souls with satisfaction when our patients get relief.

What happens, though, when we deal with patients who have problems that don't fit neatly into any category or who complain of side effects not listed in the *PDR?* Backpedaling, we retake the history, scour textbooks and, when needed, bring in consultants. Hopefully we won't let up until we find the answer. For patients, mysterious symptoms are more than puzzles to be solved. I know.

After learning that I had cancer, my oncologist explained that I had a"garden variety" of lymphoma, a fact I found reassuring because I didn't want to be "interesting" like Rita Sue. Over the subsequent months, I took comfort in knowing that my day-by-day adventure through chemotherapy was an everyday routine for my doctors and nurses.

I first tiptoed into "interesting" territory in 1994. Actually, my abdomen was the starlet when my CT scan was published alongside the results of the early-phase trials in which I was a subject. Small arrows pointed to the shrinking lymph nodes. The longer I kept outliving my prognosis, the more interesting a patient I became, in a nice sort of way.

Alas, my remarkable survival has not been all fame and fortune. Along with my growing stacks of CT scans, I have acquired a small menagerie of symptoms, some of which are, for lack of a better word, odd.

One day I decided to ask my oncologist, "Do any of your other lymphoma patients tell you they have this?" He shook his head with a sympathetic half-smile. I'm okay being the only patient my doctor has ever seen with my weirdo symptoms. I'm okay living with the symptoms, too. Even though they affect my quality of life, none are life-threatening. I really don't think much about my discomforts anymore, a reality that may be hard for healthy people to believe. Just the same, all other things being equal, I wish my oncologist *could* answer, "Yes, Wendy, quite a few of my lymphoma patients have your symptoms."

Physicians naturally exude confidence when facing familiar and treatable disease, no matter how acute the situation. Patients who fear they are imagining their symptoms (or think they are going crazy) can let go of these worries after learning their symptoms are common. They can look to their physicians, who, in turn, can dig into databases that allow projection and planning. The sense of "knowing the enemy" sows seeds of hope—the patients' and their physicians'—in the soil of options and actions, even when no known cures exist.

Being a physician-survivor has advantages: I'm skilled at detecting and describing symptoms, and I enjoy an insider's confidence in my doctors' expertise. The accuracy of my complaints is never an issue (although all my physicians keep in mind my unavoidable bias of subjectivity). I'm sure of this because my oncologist's words and actions reaffirm he knows my symptoms are real. His unfailing concern at each visit reassures me that the unsolved puzzle is important and won't be forgotten or ignored. For now, there just are no answers.

Years ago, Rita Sue got well and was discharged from the hospital without a definitive diagnosis. Her anxiety over the possibility of another event was dispelled when, more than a year later, I was reading a case report in the *New England Journal of Medicine* and enjoyed a Eureka! moment: "This is it. This is what Rita Sue had." Sure enough, we retrieved a tube of Rita Sue's frozen blood and confirmed the diagnosis. No longer "interesting," Rita Sue has remained compliant with the steps we now know can help prevent another episode.

Variety may be the spice of life, but a patient's puzzling symptoms can stir an unsettling sense of uncertainty about one's future and one's self. The longer my odd symptoms persist, the less likely they will resolve by themselves. But, who knows? Maybe they will. Maybe, as happened for Rita Sue, their cause will be uncovered and treatments discovered. I can hope. In the meantime, my oncologist keeps caring, and he keeps looking.

P.S. This morning I received an unexpected letter. "Dear Dr. Harpham. I just read an article about you. I felt like they were describing *me*! Hearing your story made me feel better. Thank you for sharing it." Her letter changes nothing about my situation. Yet adding it to my file makes me feel less alone and one patient closer to my oncologist's *Eureka!* moment regarding me. And today, that makes me feel better.

- We reassure patients by validating that we believe their unusual or inexplicable symptoms are real.
- We comfort patients by letting them know when they are not the only ones with their unusual symptom or problem.
- We help patients nourish hope by expressing confidence in our ability to manage unusual symptoms or problems.

Wrong Right Answer

The medical boards test our knowledge. It is for this knowledge that our patients come to us. But sometimes the right answer for the medical boards is the wrong answer if the same question is asked by a patient.

Walking into the auditorium, nothing prepares me for the drama about to unfold. At a plenary panel on survivorship, the assembly of specialists sits comfortably on stage, poised to share its expertise. Below, at the front of each aisle, an AV tech perches a microphone on a stand, like a t-ball coach preparing for the pitch.

I stroll in with the other survivors and find a seat. The color of my name tag and my chemo-curl mark me as a patient. Yet my perspective remains primarily that of a physician, since in my mind I'm just on temporary leave—however annoyingly prolonged—from my professional life.

After brief introductions and a series of basic questions, a middle-aged woman adjusts the microphone and then taps it twice. *Thunk. Thunk.* Everyone shushes, and she introduces her question with a two-sentence synopsis of her history: "I've been through multiple courses of treatment, including clinical trials. My cancer is progressing, and my oncologist says he has nothing else to try. What can you do for me?"

At the dais, a dance of eye contact and shoulder shrugs determines who will respond. The physician who answered the prior question slides the table microphone toward the director of palliative care, who pulls it closer and then leans in, practically kissing the mike. In measured words, he talks of shifting hopes at various points in the survivorship trajectory. Then he begins outlining excellent resources for ensuring good quality end-of-life care.

The teaching is interrupted, "That's your answer?!" the woman screeches. "I didn't ask about dying. I'm asking you..." she says, straining to sound civil, "What can you do to help me?"

"What can anyone do?" I think. Physicians can only offer what is available, while protecting patients from futile interventions.

The palliative care specialist stands up, taking the microphone with him as he walks toward the foot of the stage. It's a complex task: helping patients hear what they don't want to hear, so they can get good care.

I think back to how I responded to my patients. While ruffling through memories, I'm startled by loud voices. I look over. Some people have stood up to cheer on the woman, who's now yelling at the doctor. Others are trying to guide her away from the microphone. Throughout, the physician maintains a calm demeanor, although I sense controlled irritation (or is it exasperation?). The dialogue continues only briefly, the two talking past each other.

This fiasco leaves me shaken and feeling sad for everyone: the vulnerable patient and her supporters, and the survivors (like me) who fear we'd lose our cool but hope we'd meet our fate gracefully. I feel for the physician, too, whose reward for volunteering his time will be a dismal post-event evaluation.

How could things have gone so wrong?

The scene has stayed with me for years, challenging me to find words that help patients who refuse to believe they are out of treatment options. I realize now that the physician on the panel was handicapped, because he and the patient were strangers. And this highlights how the degree to which a physician can help may depend on how well the physician and patient know and trust each other. But even longtime patients can get upset with their doctors.

Bumping up against the limits of modern medicine is painful, and not just for the patient. With nothing left in your black bag to try to get the patient well, and with treatable and curable patients awaiting your attention in other exam rooms, it's natural to want to write off angry patients and withdraw.

This is one of the burdens of being a physician: bearing the brunt of a patient's fury, on occasion. Some motherly advice: Don't take it personally. I am not suggesting you signed up to be a punching bag. You don't have the time or energy. Besides, it's not helpful for your patient to direct unbridled anger at you. But whatever your patient says, you can't get mad back. And you can't lie.

So what's the answer? The heart of the challenge is the same as in other circumstances where patients ask for useful information when they can't process it. If a patient, hazy from anesthesia, lifts his head off the pillow to ask, "What can you do?" it's pointless to outline treatment choices. Similarly, after being told, "You have cancer," most patients don't hear another word you say that day. So you schedule a follow-up visit to discuss the next steps. In all these situations, healing words and actions help the patients return to you later, when they are ready to learn.

Compassionate care involves listening to patients' pain that can't be fixed. After acknowledging both their distress and the great divide—"I can only imagine…"—maybe offer to do some checking with colleagues around the country, "to make sure no stone has been left unturned." Or try focusing on helping them stay as healthy and comfortable as possible, because "You never know: People sometimes do better than expected." It can't hurt to state your commitment once again, "I'll always do all I can to help you, no matter what happens."

More than anything, patients who ask questions but aren't ready for the answers need reassurance that you care, that all hope is not lost, and that you won't abandon them. Dramatic encounters at the limits of knowledge emphasize the importance of trust in healing relationships.

- Our obligations to patients with unfixable problems are just as strong as our obligations to patients with treatable and curable medical problems.
- We help patients by hearing the real questions behind the questions they ask us.
- Sometimes the best answer to a patient's question is a truthful generalization that can hold him or her until such time as he or she is ready to hear the whole truth.

CHAPTER 2

Hope

"...it is not for you...to take hope from any patient..."

Sir William Osler

My fingers stroked the smooth maroon cover of my first textbook of medicine, with its luscious leather scent. I was raring to start classes and learn about all those topics listed in the lengthy index. More than anything, I wanted the power to give patients hope. And the surest way I knew to do that was with expert medical care.

My medical school instructors reinforced again and again the notion that I would not be treating diseases and injuries after graduation. No, I would be treating "people" with diseases and injuries. They hammered into me the need to tend to each patient's body *and* emotions if I wanted to deliver good care.

When I finally got to the wards, I saw this truth in action: Patients' emotions affected their medical course and quality of life. Most patients expressed fear. Many struggled with anger, anxiety or the need to feel in control. And unless I addressed these and other emotions, I risked missing the diagnosis or achieving a suboptimal outcome.

One emotion played a role in every single case: hope. Some patients had great hope of recovery while others had little. And patients' levels of hope didn't always correspond to what their medical situations seemed to merit. As I saw it, the better the patient's prognosis, the more hope of recovery there was and the more hope a patient should be feeling.

I expected better medical care to lead to better prognoses, so I tried to give my patients hope by guiding and supporting their efforts to choose and comply with optimal therapies. But it didn't always work out that way in my medical practice. Despite great effort to address my patients' negative emotions, some patients made wise choices and complied with therapies yet didn't feel hopeful. And occasionally, a patient who expressed great hope rejected my medical advice.

"This is America," I'd say to my patients. "I respect your right to choose. My job is to make sure you clearly understand your situation and your choices." Ultimately I had to let my patients decide what attitudes they'd adopt and on which therapies they'd hinge their hopes. The primary issues for me remained optimizing my patients' treatments and addressing their fears and anxieties, so they could comply with therapy; hope stayed in the background.

Not so, after I became a patient. Hope—the pleasurable feeling associated with the belief that some future good can happen (something that will bring future happiness)—became the centerpiece of my survivor-ship. Why? Because I discovered that hope was broader than the statistical projections that defined my progno-sis; it was more than how I felt about these forecasts.

In fact, the primary hope of my early survivorship—my hope for cure—faded away, replaced by other hopes, such as the hope that I'd make wise decisions and ob-tain optimal treatments. And the hope that I'd find the fortitude needed to get through treatments. Now many of my daily hopes revolve around my quality of life, re-lationships with others and purpose on earth.

As for my hope for renewed health, this has fluctu-ated through the many remissions and recurrences of my survivorship. A surprisingly wide range of factors has fueled or weakened my hopefulness: my current prognosis, of course, but also my level of fatigue, the degree of my leg pain, any news of other patients' out-comes (such as co-survivors from support group, neigh-bors and even celebrities), and how much hope the people around me have projected.

Over the years, I slowly came to appreciate the dy-namic nature and pervasive impact of hope on my life. I saw how critical it was and yet how difficult it could be to nourish many of my hopes, especially when things weren't going well. Two insights have helped me: (1) I can choose to set the stage for hope and (2) sometimes I need others' support to set the stage in any meaningful way.

Of the many sources of guidance and support I've received over the years, my doctors and nurses, along with the hospital oncology social worker, have profoundly shaped my sense of hope at certain junctures. I remember blurting out to my internist after learning of my first recurrence, "Please don't give up on me!" Oh how I wanted and needed my healthcare team to be hopeful. And they were. My doctors and nurses chose their words to convey their hope. They helped me nurture my belief in the possible good outcome whenever I was faced with discouraging statistics or difficult losses.

I've come to believe that healthcare professionals' obligations go beyond preventing and treating side effects and complications. Clinicians also have an obligation to help patients nourish hope for good things. While ordering tests and prescribing therapies, clinicians can share the words of Cicero: "While there's life, there is hope."

I won't swear that hope was never discussed in my medical school classes, but I can't recall a single mention of it. Either way, it astounds me that this essential element of patient care didn't—and still doesn't—merit a single index entry in 10-ton tomes of medicine. So this next chapter explores hope in the context of expert care. The tales will encourage you to think about the words and actions you can use to help your patients find hope.

You'll notice I didn't say you can "give" your patients hope. I now understand that hope arises from within a person, like faith or inner peace. As clinicians, all you can do is open your patients' hearts to hope for good things. And you have the power to do this in ways your patients' loving friends and devoted family cannot.

In this chapter, you'll read about the hope-crushing power of one little word—"if"—in your discussions about a patient's future. And you'll see the power of a one-word substitution to keep your answers from feeling like nails in the coffin and more like fountains of hope. A story about gambling metaphors illustrates how words can cloud or clarify the relationship between probability and luck, depending on whether we're talking about craps or poker.

We'll play the devil's advocate sometimes, taking "hope" to task. Might hope sometimes be a bad thing? Can doctors express too much hope? Do healthcare professionals have an obligation to keep not only their patients' blood pressure in a healthy range, but also their patients' hope?

We'll venture into uncomfortable territory by talking about the galloping hope associated with patients' participation in clinical trials, the rollercoaster hope patients feel when following the agony and ecstasy of sick celebrities, and the hope-challenging task of transferring patients to hospice.

All the hope-related stories reflect my belief that our professional obligations extend beyond guiding and supporting our patients' efforts to get good care. We can use the weight of our words to tip the scales and help our patients find a balance of hope and acceptance that helps them live most fully today, tomorrow, and every day.

Our mission is to preserve life. Where there is hope, there is life.

Reflections on a Haven 2007

The day I completed my ninth round of cancer treatment in November 2007, I realized in a whole new way how the pain of treatments is linked to hope.

You make me sick, y'know. So with giddy joy I'm about to bid you farewell. Sayonara. And hallelujah. No more IVs. No more pricks. No more nasty needlesticks.

Two years ago, after a deliciously long remission, my lymphoma recurred yet again. My best option was returning to you. Now, with calculated coolness, I'm strolling by the nurses' station, hoping I can get my final treatment without letting it slip that today is my last day. Please, no shower of confetti for me; let's just get this over with.

As usual, one of the nurses catches my eye and nods as if to say, "You're in." Mothers may have eyes in the back of their head, but that's nothing compared to your nurses. They monitor computer screens, incoming and outgoing visitors and patients, vital signs, emotions and, most importantly, injections and drips where a misplaced decimal can decimate.

I watch one of the younger oncologists breeze through. I'm sure I walked with the same confidence years ago in my practice, not realizing I was as close to understanding my patients' experiences as prison guards are to their charges' lives behind bars.

Kathy appears out of the drug room, ripping an alcohol-swab packet with her teeth as she approaches. She tells a short story to serenade me during the slow subcutaneous injection.

Snap. Kathy's gloves are off. My throat suddenly tightens, and my salivary glands start tingling the way they do when I'm trying not to cry. I have never felt emotional like this when I've finished treatment before.

In 1991 when the nurse took out my last IV, I felt dazed. And scared. Without you, how could I trust my body to keep the cancer at bay—the same body that had allowed the cancer to grow? Leaving you felt like leaping off a ship, with the shoreline far away.

Over the years, after each recurrence you served as the epicenter of my hope—ground zero for the match between science-based therapies and my cancer. At the end of each treatment course, my thoughts focused completely on my future: What could I do to hasten my recovery? How could I pursue happiness now, after cancer? Would I beat the odds and stay well?

"Done," Kathy announces.

I stand up and instinctively hug her. "Thanks for everything," I say, while thrusting a bag filled with gifts in her hand. "Here. These are for y'all."

"Oh! Is this your *last* treatment?"

I nod, feeling like a regular at a bar where everyone knows my name and "good-bye" means "until next time."

But I'm not thinking about if or when I'll have a "next time." I'm just glad I'm done, and I want to get out. Yet as I head straight for the door, my legs take me on a detour toward Brook, who's eyeing an IV and counting drops.

"Hey, Brook."

She looks over her shoulder.

"Bye," I say, my arms opening wide.

Brook falls in without hesitation. It's a nurse thing: No explanation necessary. Only after I let go, does she register today's "why."

"Wendy," Brook calls as I walk away. "We'll see you 'round."

"I hope not!" I blurt out without thinking.

"No, not *here*...." Brook stammers, swirling her pen in the air as if mixing cake batter in a bowl, "*Around,* with your lectures and books."

"Okay," I chuckle, choke up and keep walking.

This doesn't make sense. I've learned to live well with the uncertainty. And with my youngest child now off at college, the primary fuel for my fear of dying has slowed to a trickle. I'm less anxious about tomorrow, so why am I more emotional about finishing treatment?

Maybe it's because I'm realizing what you've done for me beyond easing my hard times and nourishing my hope of surviving: You have given me reason to believe in a future where everyone treats everyone else with kindness and patience, love and caring, and mutual respect.

You see, lately I've been struggling with increasing worries about the world in which my children will grow old, given the pressing weight of global troubles that have no resolution in sight. Yet I've never lost hope. And I believe it is partly thanks to you. Each time I've come here, I've seen people under stress working and laughing together in perfect harmony, using knowledge and technology only for good. In this space, my hoped-for possibility is a reality.

Using a voice that won't startle Amy, who's sitting with her back to me beside the patient by the door, I whisper, "Thanks for everything." Then, against my better judgment, I come up from behind and wrap my right arm around Amy's upper chest, careful not to contaminate her gloved hands. "Bye, Amy." She reciprocates the only way possible, by putting pressure on my arm with her head.

Briskly I head down the short hall to the office exit. Hundreds of times over the years, without a second thought I've pressed the little red button on the wall to unlock the door. As I reach for it today, it strikes me as funny. "What? Are you trying to slow down escapees?"

As if on cue, Amy grabs me from behind—"Was today your *last* time?"—and pulls me into her arms. She doesn't mind that I'm leaving a smudge of mascara on the shoulder of her shirt before she returns to the haven I'm leaving behind, maybe—hopefully—forever.

Moments later, I am regaining my composure as the elevator's humming crescendos into a *ding*. The doors open. I step in and don't look back.

Yeah, you make me sick. That's how you get me well. And I love you for it.

- We help patients heal by reminding them that the same treatments that make them sick offer them hope of improvement.
- Even if we are busy caring for sick patients, everyone benefits when we take a moment to say good-bye to patients who no longer need our care.
- We comfort patients by explaining that long after we stop caring *for* them, we will continue to care *about* them.

If—Not When

It's easy to sound hopeful when your patient's prognosis is good, no matter how risky or harsh the course of treatment. What about when your patient's long-term prognosis is not good? How hopeful are you when your patient is doing well but you expect this respite from illness to be temporary? How do you respond to your patient's questions about the prognosis? How hopeful would you like your patient to be?

Dr. Betty Katz hunches over the nursing station, writing orders. The clatter of a chart landing on a nearby desk catches her attention. Out of the corner of her eye, she watches a colleague fumbling with his stethoscope while slipping his cell phone in his pocket.

"Hello, Dr. Solor." Dr. Katz's distinctively dusky voice invites conversation, "And thank you for your lovely update notes on our mutual patient, Jeff. I guess you'll be seeing him soon for his follow-up?"

The young oncologist sits down and smiles timidly, still daunted by her wealth of experience and insights. "This afternoon, actually."

"Could I trouble you for a quick update? He's on my schedule for Friday. It'll help me if I know what you told him."

"Absolutely. He's had a nice response to this last round of treatment: a complete remission. Unfortunately, when his cancer recurs, it'll be aggressive. We won't be able to do much."

"If," Dr. Katz says, crisply.

"If?"

"*If* Jeff's cancer recurs." She continues without a trace of sarcasm, "If he doesn't get killed first by a Mack truck on his way to your office."

Dr. Solor grimaces. "I have no choice. At every visit, Jeff says to me, 'Doc, tell me the truth. And don't sugarcoat.' Assuming he won't get hit by a Mack truck, I'll lay out the statistics, not only out of professional obligation but also out of respect for him. After all, Jeff is a scientist."

Dr. Katz's expression remains unreadable.

"Jeff's cancer *will* recur," he repeats gently, as if unsure he was heard. "And when it does—this type always does—it's bad."

"Always? Forgive my contrariness, Dr. Solor, but *some*one *some*where survived his type of cancer."

"So?"

"So, *if*—not *when*."

"With all due respect, Dr. Katz, aren't you suggesting I encourage Jeff to hang his hope on something that rarely ever happens? Aren't you asking me to give him false hope?"

"False hope is the belief in something that is impossible. It may be unlikely that Jeff will enjoy a long remission or that a new treatment will be discovered in time, but it is possible."

"But the chances…"

"…are infinitesimally small. Believe me, I know." Dr. Katz dabs at the moistness in her eyes with the back of her wrist. "So does Jeff. I've known him since he was a grad student. As you said, Jeff is a scientist."

"That's why he expects me to be straight—scientific—about his current prognosis."

"Prognosis, not prediction. Nobody's looking to you for certainty."

"Then what?"

"The likely outcome. And what can be done, if anything." She leans her face in closer to his, "You have *some* hope, don't you?" then immediately retracts both her question and her body. "Wait!" she protests, her forearm instantly between them, arthritic fingers pointing up and palm facing forward like a policeman's signal to stop. "Don't answer that."

Lowering her hand to her lap, she asks, "Do you remember how, after Jeff's diagnosis, he was immobilized with morbid thoughts? You recommended a support group?"

He nods cautiously.

"1 saved him. Taught him how to find hope and to laugh again. Do you have two more minutes? I could tell you a quick story from a time before support groups, before pink ribbons and yellow bracelets, when the only "survivors" were relatives who lived on after loved ones died."

"I'd be honored."

"Thirty-odd years ago, I'd just passed my medicine boards when I was diagnosed with colon cancer that had spread to a local lymph node. The night after my surgery, the surgeon sat on my hospital bed and told me, 'I got it all.' But I knew that the likelihood of recurrence—and death—was high. I had two little kids at home, like our patient, Jeff. My doctor then administered the medicine that helped me through the rest of that horrific day, and the day after that, and the next day after that. He said, "Betty, you are doing well now. *If* your cancer recurs…"

She pauses before concluding, "Whatever you might be feeling yourself, you can leave space for Jeff to decide how much hope he wants to have."

Later that afternoon, Dr. Solor enters the exam room where Jeff sits expectantly. After performing a physical exam and checking the lab results, he shares the good news. As predicted, Jeff asks, "Okay Doc, what's the prognosis? Tell me the truth. And don't sugarcoat."

Dr. Solor straightens his tie and clears his throat. "As you know from your research on the Web, the usual scenario for patients in remission from this type of cancer is that the disease recurs, aggressive and hard to treat."

Jeff remains motionless.

"But unexpected, long remissions can happen. And new treatments are coming down the pike. Jeff, you are doing well now. *If* the cancer recurs, we'll deal with it."

* * *

For patients facing a high risk of recurrent or progressive disease, a physician's "when" prefaces a prediction, not a prognosis, and forces patients to choose: Either they live the rest of their days without hope, or they rail against the edict by nourishing hope against the odds and, in the process, losing some confidence in the doctor who's given up. A prediction of doom, like a terrible secret you wish you'd never been told, burdens patients with a sense of certainty that makes it far more difficult—and for some patients, impossible—to find joy.

In contrast, a prognosis preceded by "if" introduces uncertainty. This hint of possibility encourages patients to strive for a balance of hope and acceptance that helps them work and play, laugh and love in the face of a fragile future. For patients to be free to find the balance that helps them live, the door must be left open for them to find hope.

- We dignify patients by acknowledging their right to be hopeful.
- We help patients find hope by teaching them they don't have to choose between accepting a likely grim outcome and hoping for an unlikely good outcome.
- We help patients heal by helping them find a balance of hope and acceptance that helps them live fully.

Crapshoot

Our medical texts never mention "luck" as a factor in healing, yet our patients often perceive luck as playing an essential role in their medical outcomes. We do our patients a service by addressing the role of luck in healing.

Your patient sits in your office, quietly nodding as you list the risks and benefits of a particular course of treatment. When you're done, she looks you in the eye and announces her decision: "I'll pass. Even with treatment, the outcome is a crapshoot."

This sentiment peppers patients' message boards and listservs, and it troubles me. I need to explore why.

Not a gambler, I first Google "craps" to learn about the dice game behind the expression. Rolling certain numbers (such as 7 or 11) wins, and throwing other numbers loses. Assuming an honest game with legitimate dice, luck alone determines whether a player comes out richer or poorer.

Casinos don't have a monopoly on luck. In daily life everywhere, that incomprehensible and uncontrollable ethereal force is busily tipping circumstances—from trivial to momentous—for good or ill.

Years ago, when lightning struck my cousin's house and fried his surge-protected computer, he blamed bad luck. And last fall, when I drove my kids to the mall the Friday after Thanksgiving and found a lone parking space right by the entrance, we cheered our good luck. Since mystery and vulnerability (along with change and loss) define the human condition, everyone grapples with luck.

In medical contexts, a patient's luck can become the gatekeeper to optimal care. Luck gets awarded credit for the fortuitous fender bender that leads to the incidental x-ray finding of an early—and still curable—carcinoma. Luck is charged with determining the availability of a needed organ for transplant or a slot in a promising clinical trial for one desperate patient but not for another. Patients know this.

Patients recognize luck as an ever-present companion, determining the genes inherited at conception and assigning either Nurse Nightingale or Ratched at their bedside the day they die. So what's the problem with patients calling their future a crapshoot? Everything.

For starters, patients' hopefulness may be lifted or dashed by their confidence in luck, especially if they tack on a "y." Whereby people think of "luck" as a free-floating force that can impact anyone anytime, they see "being lucky" as an invisible body wrap that attracts good or bad fortune like nails to a magnet. Patients may sense, even subliminally, "I am (un)lucky, so there is (no) hope."

More worrisome is that patients might wonder why they should agree to follow-up tests or treatments if temperamental gods of fortune are calling the shots. Fatalism may lead them to resume smoking cigarettes, skip rehab or reject treatment recommendations in an effort to seize the day.

Before Lister's work in the mid-19th century, surviving puerperal fever seemed like a crapshoot. Once germ theory was proven, antisepsis replaced talismans. But advancements in science aren't enough. Explanations involving membrane receptors and pharmacodynamics won't necessarily eliminate patients' concerns about luck. Often when patients ask, "Why did this happen?" what they really want to know is "Why did this happen *to me?*"

Now I see what's been bothering me: Patients who call treatment a crapshoot may be confusing the link between probability and luck, which could lead them to downplay the power of wise choices. If things go badly, beliefs about luck or luckiness could create a burden of undeserved blame (even though the outcome is, in fact, completely in-line with probability). Most worrisome of all, such patients might turn their back on treatments that could help.

I need to start responding when the crapshoot metaphor pops up on message boards. I can explain how "Having treatment options means you don't have to depend completely on good luck to get well." Then, continuing the gambling imagery, I can offer a better metaphor: "Facing cancer—actually, living life—is like playing poker: You can't control what cards you've been dealt, but you can choose how you play your hand. And your physicians can help you play your hand well."

I can tell them how in 1993, I entered a clinical trial after my second recurrence. My husband, knowing the odds were long, encouraged me by saying, "Wendy, this trial gives you the best odds for improvement. And remember: You don't need a full house for every hand. You just need to draw an ace at the right time."

That summer I got lucky and drew an ace: The trial drug worked for me.

My husband will tell you, "Wendy helped make her luck by finding out about the trial."

And he is right. At every juncture, I've worked with my physicians to choose treatments that improved my odds, paving a path for survival. And what if I hadn't been lucky and the treatments hadn't worked for me? I'd have no regrets, comforted by the knowledge that I'd done my best.

For all our progress in medicine, much remains a mystery. As long as outcomes are unpredictable and inexplicable, luck will continue to work its charms. By clarifying the distinction between probabilities and luck, professionals help patients choose wisely. And by helping patients think about luck in healthy ways, patients' spirits will be lifted by the good will of people who wish them "Good luck."

- We help our patients by clarifying the relationship between probability and luck.
- We help patients find hope by emphasizing the power of wise treatment choices.
- We help patients nourish hope by restating our commitment to do all we can to help them accept the cards life has dealt them and to help them play their hand well.

Matzo Balls

When no curative therapies are available, patients may feel all hope for long life is lost. We help patients find hope by talking about research. Our patients can embrace the hope of clinical trials, even those patients who are not eligible to be subjects in trials.

Summer 1993. I was far from home and about to take the biggest and scariest gamble of my life. What came to mind? Matzo balls—you know, those tasty dumplings in chicken soup. I remembered how my mom hated "cannonballs," matzo balls so firm that forcing a soup spoon through the center was an art. Too much pressure on an improperly angled spoon sent those dumplings flying.

Mom's goal was "fluffy." For 40 years, she had occasional successes, but mostly failures that she attributed to the moon or the weather or the importance of the guests at the dinner table. In Mom's search for the right recipe, the soup tureen became my Sabbath lotto draw: What would the matzo balls be this week?

Until that summer, my approach to choosing treatment had always been to lean on statistics to stack the odds in my favor. Yet there I was, flying off to Stanford University Medical Center to participate in a clinical trial designed to determine the risks of a new cancer therapy. One of the consulting oncologists from another institution chided me for playing Russian roulette by becoming the 15th and last person to enter the Phase I trial of monoclonal antibodies.

Why was I pursuing a treatment with so many unknowns? Because my lymphoma—an indolent form that every oncology textbook deemed incurable—had recurred twice since my diagnosis two-and-a-half years earlier. Because no standard therapy offered me a realistic hope of a durable remission, let alone cure. Because I had three young children at home. And because the day after a night of fervent prayer—"Thy will be done, but could you leave me a clue or two?"—I was notified by the researcher at Stanford that the clinical monitors approved my eligibility for the trial.

Pursuing what my local doctors and I believed to be my best option was still difficult. It meant letting go of my hope of finding a definite "right" answer. It meant hinging my hope on the unknown.

When the West Coast nurses hooked me up to an IV and started the infusion of the investigational drug, my husband and I held our breath. The uncertainty was excruciating. And that's when I thought of Mom's matzo balls: What would the lymph nodes be this week?

The treatment was relatively easy, although we all became anxious when I developed nausea and faintness due to low blood pressure an hour into the infusion. My symptoms resolved with medication and intravenous fluids, but the idea that something unexpected *could* go wrong kept us on edge.

That evening I was discharged. Since it was late, my husband and I decided to stop for dinner on the way back to the hotel. Picture this: sizzling steaks, steaming baked potatoes, salad and, of course, fresh, hot, San Francisco sourdough bread. To others we must have appeared like an average middle-aged couple out to dinner. To us it was anything but ordinary. Feeling normal after treatment was eerie. Recalling my past attempts at dinner after chemotherapy, my husband and I both kept thinking, "Could one single treatment that didn't make me bald or sick really get rid of malignant lymphoma? Could we hope for a remission? For a cure?" I imagine that my emotions were not unlike those felt by the first patients to receive penicillin and recover quickly and completely from serious infections, instead of dying, as did most people before antibiotics.

By the end of the trial, my cancer had responded. Not completely, and not for long. But my partial remission lasting eight months was significant enough to justify more trials. Over the subsequent four years, in addition to another nine-month course of chemotherapy, I received the same novel antibody therapy in two more clinical trials. A year after I participated in the third trial, my cancer recurred—again. By this time, the trial drug had been FDA-approved and marketed as Rituxan.

Compared to my stormy first winter with cancer back in 1990, my recurrence in the spring of '98 was a breeze: Every Tuesday for four weeks, I stopped at a local deli to buy a Styrofoam cup filled with matzo ball soup (not as good as my mother's, of course) and then drove to my oncologist's office. The Rituxan attacked the lymphoma, the salty chicken broth fixed the drop in blood pressure, and the matzo ball comforted the little girl in me who didn't like being sick.

I told you how entering the trial reminded me of waiting for the Friday evening verdict on my mom's matzo balls. A well-executed clinical trial of cancer treatment can feel like a lotto drawing because nobody knows the answer until the numbers roll out. But there the similarity ends. Good quality research is based not on chance or anecdote but on sound science, the modern tool for discovering truths about treating cancer.

The textbooks are wrong: As long as there is research, my type of lymphoma is not incurable; it is one of the types for which scientists are working toward a cure. While researchers keep looking, I'm busy living my life—a good life—a life I have because a few years ago research produced a treatment for lymphoma that works well for me.

While current treatments keep my lymphoma at bay for now, I tell Joe ongoing trials give me hope for tomorrow.

And oh, by the way, years ago my mother solved her little problem: She learned to add seltzer instead of water to the batter. Perfect matzo balls every time.

- When curative therapies are not available, we help patients who are not in trials by explaining that standard therapies may keep them well long enough to benefit from better remedies that come along.
- We guide patients to wise treatment decisions by pointing out that hope based on science is stronger than that based on wishful thinking.
- We help patients find hope by reminding them that no disease is incurable, because researchers are working toward a cure.

The Risk of Hope

The survivor's dictum, "Choose hope," encourages patients to find hope in otherwise overwhelming circumstances. And today's culture of positive thinking halos clinicians who strive to nourish their patients' hopes. But like many ideas born of passionate benevolence, a hopeful stance can lead to disaster.

After answering the final question from the audience, I start gathering my lecture notes. One cardiology fellow hangs back until everyone else has left the auditorium. Then he approaches me, clears his throat and says, "Dr. Harpham, may I ask you a question?"

The young doctor's hesitation and furrowed brow telegraph that he isn't about to compliment my presentation.

"Throughout your lecture, you kept emphasizing the importance of hope. Sometimes, can't hope be bad?"

"In what way?" I ask.

"We recently treated an elderly woman with chronic CHF following a massive MI. The attending physician kept trying one treatment after another, reassuring the family, 'I haven't given up hope.'"

"And?"

"The patient died, and the family lashed out."

Suddenly afraid he's maligned a respected physician, the fellow quickly adds, "This guy is a superb cardiologist: sharp and up-to-date, very dedicated, self-sacrificing and caring."

I nod, sensing his meaning: a physicians' physician, the "Go-to Doc" when others tell a patient, "Get things in order."

The young man sounds agitated when he says, "All the nurses and house staff knew this patient was dying." He then imitates how the patient's family yelled, "Why did you let us have hope? You led us to believe Mother would recover."

I open my mouth to respond, but he continues, "Nowadays, all patients ever talk about is hope, hope,

hope. Well, in this case, I think hope made things worse." Quietly he mumbles, "Even the word—'hope'—now leaves a bitter taste."

I'm used to nurses complaining about doctors who hide behind the statistics and never mention hope. I cringe whenever I see patients despairing because their doctors, assuming a posture of certainty, extinguish hope. After years of writing and talking about hope, this is the first time someone suggests a problem with too much hope. Mentally replaying my lecture, I fast-forward to my comments about hope: "Myriad factors affect your patient's hopes, not the least of which is the prognosis."

I remember segueing into the paradox of competing obligations: Doctors and nurses are obligated to be truthful; at the same time, they are obligated never to extinguish hope. Then I asked the young doctors, "If remission is unlikely or death is imminent, can you be both honest and hopeful?"

After pausing to give them time to think, I delivered the punch line, "Yes, by separating expectation and hope."

Expectation is the outcome you think will happen. Hope is the outcome you want to happen and believe is possible, even if unlikely. People can expect one thing and hope for another. When my long-term prognosis was bad, I learned that I could expect to die of my lymphoma or some complication of treatment and, at the same time, I could hope for a durable remission, if not cure.

This insight arose after talking with survivors who felt hopeless because, as I saw it, they'd collapsed together expectation and hope. When the prognosis is dismal, patients seemed to lose hope more easily if their physicians discussed only the expected outcome. So I suggested to my audience of clinicians, "Share both your expectations and your hopes with your patients."

I offer my hand to my young colleague, "Thank you for your provocative question, Dr...?"

"Please call me Joe," he says as he shakes my hand and relaxes.

"Joe, I've met so many patients who, having heard nothing hopeful in their doctor's office, mistakenly think their physicians have absolutely no hope or, indeed, their situation is hopeless. This hopelessness causes great suffering."

"I understand," Joe responds. "But after what happened to that doctor, I'm worried that sharing my hopes will lead patients to conclude things are more hopeful than they are. I'd hate to get sued by a family if, as expected, a patient dies."

Joe paints a picture in which the reverberations of a doctor's hope—the same hope that sustains a family through crisis after crisis—overwhelm all evidence of imminent death. He concludes, "The problem is that people desperately want and need to have hope."

I think back to some of the terminally ill patients in my practice and how I relied on reality—the patient's obviously deteriorating condition—to help everyone keep things in perspective. The patient's physical wasting, clouded consciousness and, at the end, death rattle helped families expect and adjust to what was happening. But with today's supportive therapies routinely bringing patients back from the brink, it is not far-fetched for patients and their families to keep waiting for a rescue until the patient is cold.

I say, "Healing begins when doctors clearly separate their expectations from their hopes, and then share both with their patients. But it probably requires more."

Joe wonders aloud, "Should the message be about guiding patients to a healthy balance of expectation and hope?"

"What constitutes a healthy balance?"

Joe looks stymied.

"As both a physician and a patient, Joe, I've seen how whichever particular hope a patient might hold onto depends on which hope helps him or her live fully, especially at the end of life."

"I'm not sure I know what you mean."

"Well, I've seen patients find peace and happiness in their last days by letting go of all hope of recovery and, instead, hoping for comfort and loving-kindness as they slip away. I have also seen patients find happiness by preparing for the end and then keeping their hope full throttle. To their dying breath, they hold tight to their comforting hope for a cure."

"So you are saying that my job is to separate expectation and hope…"

"Yes," I respond, pleased. "And then you can encourage your patients to use both to help them find peace and pursue happiness."

- We comfort patients by reminding them that every member of the healthcare team is always hoping for the best possible outcome.
- We foster hope by telling patients that we are prepared to care for them through the likely outcome and are hoping they make an unexpected and inexplicable recovery that proves our prognosis wrong.
- We help patients (and ourselves) heal by encouraging everyone to find a unique balance of hope and acceptance that works well for him or her, whatever levels that might be.

The "H" Word

One of the most difficult transitions for us occurs when all treatment options have been exhausted and a transfer to hospice or other end-of-life-care setting is indicated. Many patients and their caregivers may try to avoid talking about it, shutting down your attempts to discuss it. How can you refer patients to hospice and still nourish their hope?

"Dr. Katz. Just the person I was hoping to see."

After one last little push to line up her patient's chart flush with the others, Dr. Katz cheerfully turns to her young colleague. "Ah, Dr. Solor. Just the person *I* was hoping to see. Nice pick up this morning on Mr. Mavel's hyperparathyroidism."

Dr. Solor's seriousness clashes with her compliment and the colorful decorations at the nursing station. "I've got a dilemma and could use your advice."

Pointing to two empty chairs, Dr. Katz lowers herself into the nearer one as gravity undoes her smile. This isn't the first time the young oncologist has sought her out when troubled by a situation with a patient.

"It's been a few months, but do you remember the time you and I talked about..." Dr. Solor hesitates, searching for the phrase. "How did you put it...'leaving space' for patients to find hope?"

"Sure, I remember. We were discussing our mutual patient, Jeff, right?"

He nods. "I remember your saying, 'Patients need to find a balance of hope and acceptance that works well for them.'"

She uh-hums her affirmation.

"I have another patient who, when he first came to me, told me he needed a doctor who wouldn't give up hope, no matter how bleak the situation. Well, I saw him in the clinic yesterday to discuss his recent scan results. Unfortunately, his cancer marches on no matter what I hit it with. I'm out of treatment options."

"You're at a turning point."

"Yes. I won't prescribe another treatment just so he can feel hopeful. I can't do that."

"So the problem is...?"

"He needs hospice," Dr. Solor says.

"What happened when you discussed it?"

"I...uh...didn't," Dr. Solor responds, shifting in his seat. "During his last hospitalization, his wife approached me alone at the nursing station. She sensed his latest chemo wasn't working and warned me, 'Don't even mention the "H" word to him.'"

"The 'H' word," Dr. Katz repeats. "Hotel Hopeless. Hallway to Heaven. I've heard it all."

Dr. Solor nods appreciatively. "I'm afraid that talking about hospice would extinguish all hope. I can't do that, either."

"You're right. It's a delicate undertaking to shift from care intended to prolong life to care focused primarily on quality of life."

"…and to do it without destroying hope. That's my dilemma."

"A few months ago you offered your patient chemo—with all its associated risks and discomforts—as the most hopeful approach. Can you offer him hospice as the most hopeful approach now?"

"But the two situations aren't comparable. Prescribing chemotherapy furthered our shared mission: to help the patient live. I feel as if referring him to hospice abandons our mission. I would no longer be helping him live; I'd be helping him…"

"…live," Dr. Katz interrupts, drowning out Dr. Solor's conclusion.

"Well, maybe figuratively speaking. But my patient wants to live, in the literal sense of the word. Without any hope of recovery, how could he hope to live literally or figuratively?

"In other words, you're saying that since accepting hospice means facing the likelihood of death and letting go of the hopes nurtured by cancer treatment, a referral to hospice will necessarily extinguish all his hope?"

"Won't it?"

"We are treading on thorny territory." Dr. Katz thinks for a moment before continuing. "Even when recommending hospice, I think you can leave space for hope."

"How? I'd essentially be telling him I expect him to die within six months. What hope could he—or I—possibly have?"

"For a new treatment to become available? For the prognosis to be wrong?" Dr. Katz responds and then takes a breath before continuing. "As you know, some patients do unexpectedly well when the toxicity of chemotherapy or radiation is removed. Not uncommonly, patients live longer than predicted. And, on occasion, the patient is discharged from hospice to resume active treatment."

After another brief silence, Dr. Katz continues, "It's easy to get tripped up by thinking of hope too narrowly. Along with hope for recovery, patients also hope we'll keep them comfortable and help them live better."

"Of course. But what if, as expected, my patient's condition worsens?" Dr. Solor asks.

"Many patients, maybe most patients, nurture other hopes and discover new hopes as their hope for recovery fades. I never cease to marvel over patients' ability to adapt to changing circumstances and to continually find a new balance of hope and acceptance that helps them live."

Dr. Solor remains seated, trying to absorb it all and realizing there are no quick or easy answers.

> - Physicians who shy away from discussions of hospice unwittingly deny patients the services of caregivers who can help patients prepare for and deal with dying.
> - We nourish patients' hope by teaching them recovery is possible in hospice, even if only temporarily.
> - By making referrals to hospice, we help patients nourish hope for being at home (where they are more in control of their lives), for dignity and serenity, for meaningful interchange with loved ones, and for whatever other hopes grow large as their lives wind down.

Lookin' Good

As a physician, I was always far more invested in my intellect than my appearance. So after my diagnosis it came as a bit of a surprise how much attention people paid to how I looked. In "Misunderstanding Physicians," I discuss how telling our patients "I understand" can cause unintended problems. In this piece, I illustrate how our efforts to encourage patients may backfire when we say, "You are lookin' good."

Estée Lauder, watch out: Chemo does wonders for the complexion. What else could explain why everywhere I go people tell me, "You're lookin' good"?

As a doctor in a busy solo practice, my cosmetic repertoire consisted of two sweeps of cheek blush and an application of lipstick in the morning, with a fresh coat of lipstick applied periodically throughout the day.

My appearance was a non-issue, even after dropping to my ideal weight within weeks of delivering each of my babies. (Nursing and working full-time will do that.) In fact, I remember teasing that I might as well grow a beard, since people no longer said, "Hi, how are you?" but "Hey, how's that new baby?"

In a goofy mood one evening, I teased with a girl-friend that nobody would notice if I answered, "The baby is great. I have cancer, but the baby is great. Thanks for asking." Needless to say, it wasn't funny at all when the following year it was true.

During the months of chemo that followed, I went to Internal Medicine Grand Rounds whenever my blood counts were adequate. Hoping to stay connected to the hospital scene while on medical leave, I was nervous about the attention. The first few times people said, "Wendy, you're lookin' good," I finished their greeting in my head, "...for a cancer patient on chemo," while discreetly adjusting my wig.

Week after week, compassionate colleagues went out of their way to chat and check on how my treatments were going. Invariably as they were leaving, they'd say, "You're lookin' good." And I believed them.

Why not? My colorful headscarves and dangly ear-rings along with some tricks from a beauty book for chemo-gals could work for me. I may have felt crummy, but, by golly, at least I was lookin' good.

After finishing my chemo-and-steroid cocktails, my chipmunk cheeks melted away. Before long I had some hair—eyebrows and eyelashes, too—and enjoyed wearing my white coat again.

When the same caring colleagues now saw me at conference and exclaimed with evident relief, "Wendy, you are looking sooo much better," my reality tester went kaplooey: "Better?"

Only momentarily miffed, I smiled at my gullibility and appreciated their efforts. Whether I'm in treatment or not, I like the encouragement.

But not everyone feels the same way. Reactions can be vehement, as I discovered recently while eating lunch with survivors who were griping about stupid things people say.

One survivor complained, "They shouldn't tell me I look good when I know I look like crap."

Another responded, "Yeah. If they tell me I look good, I wonder why I don't feel better than I do."

A third piped in, "They say it to shut me up. Just tell me I look good to head off hearing how tired and nauseated I am or that I'm hurting." This last comment set off serious head-nodding around the table.

Justified or not, "lookin' good" can be an emotionally charged phrase for women—and, I suppose, for men, too. Especially if said by their physicians.

As happens with innocent facial expressions, patients often imbue their physicians' every comment—even meaningless social repartee—with significant hidden messages or medical implications.

A cheery, "You're lookin' good," at the end of an office visit can cause patients to feel alienated after confiding their misery. They may feel misunderstood or not heard.

The intended reassurance can lead to patients' confusion or feelings of insecurity. Patients may wonder if they have been misjudging their symptoms. As they see it, their doctors know their test results and, presumably, know how they should be feeling. Or patients may worry about having come across as weenie whiners (or that they are, in fact, as weak and pathetic as they fear).

A physician's throwaway comment can impact patients' hopefulness, too. "You're lookin' good" may inadvertently lead patients to assume that their current state of ill-health is the best they can hope for from now on. Conversely, patients may mistakenly believe that their cancer situation or prognosis is better than what they'd correctly understood from past conversations.

Of course, it is just as possible for the intended pick-me-up to do just that: lift the patient's spirits. Whether by helping an optimistic patient get through a tough moment or by sparking hope that rescues a patient from despair, "You're lookin' good" may be exactly what the patient needs to hear.

The social instinct to sound encouraging is powerful. Recently I was visiting a friend who was slogging through a rough spot. After talking briefly about his challenges, I said without thinking, "Well, you're lookin' good." Immediately I wanted to take it back, since he didn't look well and I knew he didn't feel well.

As with all clinician-patient communications, a little clarification goes a long way. To help prevent a mismatch between what is intended and what is heard, physicians can specify: "Your situation—or progress, pain control, lab work, latest scan, whatever—is lookin' good." And they can validate patients' many challenges while offering encouragement.

How did I react when my oncologist told me I was looking good (as opposed to my reaction to my colleagues, who were relating to me socially)? Let's see…I can't remember his ever saying it. If he did, it didn't make a lasting impression one way or the other.

But I have a few pictures from my chemo days. In my favorite, I'm wearing a fuchsia scarf and a hint of lipstick, and I'm hugging my four-year-old birthday girl. If I do say so myself, I was lookin' good.

- Clinicians help patients by knowing when it helps or hurts someone who is going through—or has gone through—difficult times to hear, "You're lookin' good."
- We help patients by clarifying when we are giving a technical, medical assessment or are just relating socially.
- Friendly encouragement helps patients take proper action, so we shouldn't hesitate to share our perception if a patient is doing well and, indeed, looks good to us.

Star Power

We keep People magazines in our reception rooms for their entertainment value. But patients may find or lose hope after reading about celebrities' illnesses or deaths. Since many patients look to stars for inspiration, we need to know what our patients are learning and take advantage of star-studded teachable moments.

"The cancer freed me. It freed me," wrote Paul Tsongas about his lymphoma in a May 1992 New York Times editorial. Political pundits questioned this, two months after the senator's withdrawal from the presidential race. I took him at his word.

With my first annual post-chemo evaluation fast approaching, I eagerly continued reading Tsongas' editorial: "I have learned how to live. And to count each day. And to value that day. I am beyond terror because I have had more than enough of it."

Wow. Beyond terror. The notion was music to my ears.

Tsongas' buff-for-50 physique and forward-looking confidence gave me hope that my fatigue and frequent respiratory infections would abate. He was daring to use the other "C" word—cure—since he had been cancer-free for five years. When asked, he brushed off the radiation of a single enlarged axillary lymph node less than a year after his bone marrow transplant as "insignificant." By reassuring his supporters about his health, he quieted my anxiety about mine. In an ironic twist of fate, a single lymph node popped up in my neck later that same month.

While I was closing my medical practice and undergoing more cancer treatments, a public brouhaha was playing out in the papers over the misrepresentation of Tsongas' cancer history and prognosis. I tried to make sense of it: "What does it mean for him? For me?"

Opening the morning paper to 32-point font head-lines about Tsongas caught my eye and imagination in a way hearing about neighbors or friends-of-friends didn't. Five months later, the news was bad: Tsongas' cancer recurred. Again.

Anytime a celebrity joins the cancer club, weekly news magazines run reader-friendly reviews of state-of-the-art treatments. Fashion magazines and *People* cover the human interest side. And like an annoying little brother, tabloids dive in and splash across their front pages ghastly photos to support dire predictions.

Today's patients are privy to close-up views of celebrity survivors, sometimes closer than if it were a sibling who was sick. In a paparazzi flash, everyone is talking about "our" medical and emotional challenges in public. For the most part, this is a good thing.

It hasn't always been this way. In 1974, First Lady Betty Ford opened the door by talking about her breast cancer. Survivors everywhere applauded her courage, crediting her with smashing taboos that burdened patients with feelings of alienation and shame.

Then researchers documented a dramatic rise in detection rates of breast cancer and other types of cancer, too. Healthcare professionals were thrilled. Happily, this "Betty Ford blip" was only the first of a series of celebrity-generated eponymous factors affecting patient care, such as the "Couric" effect on colon cancer screening following Katie's televised colonoscopy.

Bigger-than-life, stars inspire philanthropists and patients with their triumphs over adversity. Many leaps in survivorship have occurred thanks to star power raising awareness and generating funding.

But the plot thickens.

Most worrisome for me is when adoring fans—our patients—look to Dr. Phil for their second opinion or follow their stars to Mexico for ineffective treatments. It happens.

Less dramatic but still important, problems can arise when patients feel connected to stars who share their diagnosis. For one thing, celebrities are not ordinary people, even if they do put on one pant (or pantyhose) leg at a time. Few stars hesitate to splurge on weekend getaways between treatment rounds, let alone worry if they can afford their life-saving treatments.

For another, celebs are pros with a practiced public face protecting their marketability. So although they may display shock when newly diagnosed, you'd be hard-pressed to find one appearing glum or hopeless during the months of treatment that follow.

What patients see are the thumbs-up pose for the hospital-discharge photo op and the glamorous (if airbrushed) return to the red carpet. Invariably some patients glance from their TV to their mirror and wonder why they don't look so hot, much the way some healthy women who wear size 8 feel fat after watching *Project Runway*.

If treatments are rocky or if things aren't going to get better, celebrities often disappear. Patients wonder what is happening, until the paper runs a story on their star's comeback show—or his or her obituary. The death of a star is more than news; it can snuff out patients' hope for themselves, given the real and perceived advantages of fame and fortune.

Am I suggesting you start TIVO-ing *Entertainment Tonight?* No. But keeping up with celebrities can help you in the care of some of your patients. You can share star-studded public service announcements that motivate your patients to proper action. Your office can provide FAQ sheets on diagnoses in the news (to staff, if not to patients). It's a fast and easy way to capitalize on golden teaching moments.

For patients who are feeling inadequate next to glossies of stars, remind them that professional makeup and camera crews can make anyone look like a million bucks. As for those patients who are feeling distraught by a broadly publicized death, validate their reaction as normal and understandable. Then reassure them: "Your course is not linked to a star, even if you do share the same diagnosis."

The day Tsongas died, I cried. And not because I thought I was doomed.

Paul Tsongas is one of my heroes. His front-and-center dance with mortality did a number on the stigma and myth surrounding cancer. With Astaire-like grace and presidential leadership, he showed me that life is what you make it.

When asked to what he credited his relentless drive to help Americans, Tsongas often answered by describing his "obligation to his survivorship." Every day I am inspired by and grateful for Tsongas and the many other celebrity-survivors who recognize their power and use it for the good of others. Bravo.

- We can guide patients away from bogus therapies being pursued by celebrities and help them separate from celebrities who are doing poorly.
- We help patients find hope by exposing myths perpetuated by celebrities.
- We strengthen hopeful messages by referring to celebrities who are promoting our messages.

Patient Patients

Every day we order blood tests and scans. The test results arrive at our offices while we are busily caring for other patients. Between patients, we skim patients' test results, screening for problems that might require urgent intervention. Most times, the test results sit on our desks until we (or our staff) can break away to notify waiting patients of their test results. Even if we are working as efficiently as humanly possible, delays between ordering a test and relaying the results are unavoidable. Still, we can make the wait easier for our patients.

The tests are done. *I'm not going to "wait and see" but "live and see."* If I've learned anything, it's that I don't have to let fear steal otherwise good time while waiting for test results. I've planned work projects and fun outings to keep me from sitting by the phone, wringing my hands.

The first few days I hardly worry at all. I may wonder occasionally if the radiology report has made it to my doctor's office yet. I may flush with a fleeting image of getting bad news. But I let these thoughts fly out of my mind as quickly as they fly in.

Another day passes. Soon I'll know whether I'm fine or if…no, I won't go there. *I don't have a problem until they tell me I have a problem.*

I envy my friend, Nate, who remains calm while waiting for the results of a second biopsy after the first one was non-diagnostic. Retrieving Nate's email from earlier this week, I read it again:

"It is what it is. Nothing I think, feel, do or say can change the results. Worrying now won't make it any easier if I do get bad news. And I'll have wasted a perfectly good day worrying for nothing if it turns out the news is good. So I'm not worrying. I guess that makes me a patient patient! Ha, ha."

All morning I try to be a patient patient. But by lunchtime, I'm picking up the receiver periodically to double-check the dial tone. Replacing my wall clock battery with a new one doesn't make the minute hand move any faster.

The squeaky wheel may get the grease, but I can't risk being a thorn in my doctor's side. I have an idea: If I don't hear from them in the next two hours, then I'll call. Five minutes later, I pick up the phone, dial my doctor's number and hang up.

I pick up my phone again and hit speed-dial 7. "Nate? How are you staying so calm? My head is starting to do crazy things, like…"

"Calm? I'm climbing the walls. Forget my last email. The longer I don't hear anything, the more convinced I am that I'm going to get bad news."

"Nate, you told me, 'No news is good news.' You said if it's bad, they call right away. I mean, they'd want to move quickly if my scan is bad, right?" Suddenly I'm queasy with worries about my cancer growing while I'm sitting here twiddling my thumbs.

Nate responds, "All I know is that I almost bit off my sister's head for calling to see if I'd heard anything."

I smile. "When I was still pregnant after my due date with my first kid, people drove me nuts calling to see if I'd had the baby. For the entire nine months of my next pregnancy, I told everyone my due date was ten days later than the official date. Worked like a charm."

"Sneaky," Nate says with chuckle, "but good."

Nate and I commiserate. The inconveniences and discomforts of the tests themselves are nothing compared to the waiting. Nighttime is the worst: In the dark and quiet, with our imaginations unleashed, any aches grow large. Talking helps me know I'm not the only patient unhinged by the helplessness of waiting.

My call-waiting signal interrupts us. "Nate, that might be him. I gotta go."

(Quick deep breath) "Hello? Oh hi, doctor. Yes, this is a perfect time."

* * *

This is not my story but a composite based on conversations with other survivors. For many patients, the lag between completing diagnostic tests and learning their results is a most stressful time. Prolonged waiting exacerbates survivors' sense of vulnerability and loss of control.

No physician or nurse can be everything to every patient all the time. Even in boutique practices, sick patients must take priority over call-backs. And ramping up to crisis mode all day is not an answer, either. You'd sacrifice the calming chitchat that enhances doctor-patient relationships and miss opportunities for healing your patients, not to mention you'd burn out quicker than birch wood on a fire.

Patients understand this. Yet patients still get upset or worry, often unnecessarily, while waiting. So consider assigning a realistic call back date. Be specific. And invite patients to call before that date if they want. The few who do call need your boost of support.

You can quash unfounded fears up front with direct reassurances. For example, "One to two weeks will make no difference in your treatment choices or how you do." And you can offer uplifting mantras, such as those italicized in the story above. Recognize that such self-talk and positive thinking can hold off the demons only so long.

Offer short-term anxiolytics and/or sedative hypnotics as a backup, if appropriate. Many patients benefit from a prescription, even if it remains unfilled—or filled but unopened—on their nightstand.

Finally, when calling with test results, thank patients for waiting and apologize for undue delays.

Tick tock. Tick tock. Waiting for test results can be trying. When it isn't possible or reasonable to review test results soon, you help your patients by guiding and supporting them through the waiting.

- You help patients cope with the waiting by assigning specific—and realistic—call back dates and inviting patients to call anytime. Patients feel respected when we thank our patients for waiting and apologize for undue delays.
- We comfort patients by providing clear reassurance that the necessary delay is medically safe.
- We help many patients by offering short-term anxiolytics and/or sedative hypnotics as a backup, if appropriate.

CHAPTER 3

Action

> *"Facts alone will not be of much service to you unless studied in connection with others and with the phenomena displayed during life."*
>
> Sir William Osler

In medical school we learn how to prevent and treat patients' injuries and illnesses. Then in practice we impress on patients the importance of complying with their prescribed health measures. But when it comes to life as a patient, knowing what to do and actually doing it are two entirely different matters.

As part of my canned new-patient spiel in my medical practice, I always said, "I can't call all my patients every evening to check on them. So I am depending on you to call me if you develop any changes or problems."

My office staff and I bent over backwards to educate our patients at every visit, sending them home with a handwritten list of the signs and symptoms for which they should call me day or night. And I reassured each of them, "I'd rather you wake me up at 2 a.m. to take care of your fixable problem than have you wait until my office opens in the morning with what could then be a less-easily treatable and even life-threatening problem, okay?"

I didn't see how I could make it any easier. So you can imagine my exasperation when one of my favorite patients, a genteel septuagenarian with ischemic heart disease, called the office to report crushing chest pain that had begun in the middle of the night. "I didn't want to bother you," she said meekly in the cardiac care unit. Aargh.

My sense of helplessness resurfaced periodically, such as the day a patient reported blood in his stool that had begun a few months earlier. He justified his delay, "I figured I'd tell you at my annual exam." As for my reaction on learning that a patient—a cancer survivor who had landed on the good side of terrible odds—had taken up smoking again, saying I was shocked would be an understatement. Sure, I respected patient autonomy. And I wasn't expecting perfection. Yet I couldn't shake the feeling that these patients' irresponsibility was my failing. I kept looking for steps I could take to narrow the gap between patients knowing what to do and actually doing it. But I had no idea what I could say or do. Until I became a patient.

From the moment of my diagnosis, I had a better-than-average understanding of what to do and why. Naturally, I was invested in becoming a "good" patient. If I did everything perfectly, I'd have the best chance of recovery with minimal complications. And these were my colleagues—my friends—caring for me. I wanted to make their job easier.

Yet just days after my original diagnosis, I disobeyed doctor's orders. Despite clear instructions from my surgeon not to lift anything heavier than 15 pounds, when my big-boy 22-month-old fell and started crying, I ran and picked him up. I kept carrying and comforting him until my husband saw us and ever-so-gently yelled at me.

More than a few times during that first year, I hesitated to do what I knew to be the right thing. Sometimes I went through contortions, needing my husband or friends to hold me accountable before I would take proper action. These experiences opened my eyes to the difficulties patients face when it comes to taking action.

In this chapter, we'll explore words that might help patients overcome the many obstacles to acting on their knowledge in healthy ways. In "Beginning?" we'll explore the difficulties of calling for an appointment or coming in after developing a new symptom. Then we'll take a look at the bane of schedulers: missed appointments.

With "I'm tired" being a common chief complaint of patients, I'll share some mantras that have helped me as I've dealt with post-cancer fatigue. This way while you are evaluating for treatable causes of fatigue, you can send patients home with a plan of action for dealing with it.

Between office visits and hospitalizations, many patients are inundated with unsolicited advice about mind-body connections, diets, over-the-counter preparations and alternative therapies from family, friends and even strangers. So I'll talk about helping patients who want to use visualization in their recovery and patients who are afraid that drinking a Coca-Cola will kill them. I'll conclude this chapter with a think piece about placebos, because patients who are unhappy with watchful waiting often push their doctors to "do something."

Beginning?

As I rushed from one exam room to the next, I'd take a second or two to clear my head before beginning another patient encounter. With as much calm and focus as I could muster quickly, I'd then enter the room ready to begin. What I didn't realize was that it wasn't the beginning at all.

On my return from morning rounds, my receptionist was scribbling a patient's name in the office schedule. She glanced at me and rolled her eyes, mouthing the ETA of the add-on, one of my "regulars." When the time came, I skimmed my patient's chart before knocking to announce my entrance. Reaching for the doorknob, I took a cleansing breath and geared up, "On your mark, get set, go!"

Every office encounter was a puzzle, no matter how familiar the patient or the complaints. But unlike a relaxing crossword or jigsaw, the problems were pressing and the goal was serious: healing my patient as efficiently and painlessly as possible, for both the patient's sake and mine.

With cleared head and hopeful heart, I opened the exam room door and scanned my patient for clues such as pallor or splinting. And so I began one more modern quest for healing. But was it really the beginning? After I became a cancer patient, I realized how self-centered—how wrong—I'd been.

Such quests actually begin much earlier, prompted by an impersonal, dispassionate fact, such as a new lump or pain. Sooner or later the patient becomes aware of the change. "Hmm, what's this? Was this here before?" For patients in remission from MS, cancer or other relapsing disease, this simple awareness instantly becomes something totally different. "What does this lump mean? What's causing my pain? Could my disease be back? Could it be worse than before?"

Just for a moment, imagine walking into your home to find your living room ransacked. Within seconds you'd call 911. But what if you found one lamp knocked over or your easy chair facing the wrong direction, enough of a difference to catch your attention yet not enough to inconvenience you? For patients, it's the skin rashes, lumps and aches that are not particularly dramatic or debilitating that can pose the greatest challenge between scheduled office visits. "Is this real? Is it just a minor blip, a normal 'nothing'? Okay to ignore? Or do I need to do something about it?"

If the symptom persists, or goes away only to recur, patients may find themselves slipping on a slick of barbed questions and memories: "What else could it be? What will we do if it is a relapse?" Scans. Biopsies. Telling people. Decisions about treatment. Clinic visits and hospital stays. Medical bills. Stress.

"Maybe if I wait a little longer, it'll go away" is a possibility that offers patients refuge. For many, hope becomes reality and the unreported scare is forgotten.

For others, the symptom persists until the patient crosses a psychic threshold (or a loved one insists), "This needs medical attention."

Good. The patient has decided the symptom needs evaluation. Now what? If given a written exam, the patient undoubtedly and without hesitation would check the correct answer: "Call my doctor's office." But knowing what to do and doing it are two completely different matters. Minds play games like "I don't have time. What about my commitments? My plans?" Patients know too well how life can get complicated and stressful when illness usurps the top of the To-Do list.

The practical issues are often minor obstacles compared with the emotional ones, especially on weekends, when physicians' offices are closed. "I don't want to bother my doctor with something that really could have—should have—waited. But I don't want to wait with something that needs immediate attention." Memories of exam rooms and treatment suites open doors for demons bent on stirring up primal fears: "If I call the doctor, it means it might be something serious. If I go in, they might find something bad. If they find something bad, I'll be a patient—vulnerable and out-of-control—again.

Like an exhausted child who wails, "I am NOT tired. I don't need to go to sleep!," responsible, intelligent people may deny what they know and reject actions that help because... well, they don't want to be sick.

When it comes to helping our patients heal, how could I think even for a second that the physician's entry into the equation ever marks the beginning? What hubris. On that morning years ago, by the time I'd buttoned my starched white coat and opened the exam room door, my patient already had noted the sign or symptom, determined that it might signal a problem that needed my evaluation, and then found the wisdom and strength to overcome all the obstacles to making an appointment and keeping it.

Even in cases when I was the first professional to see the patient, I was a second-line player, assisting the efforts of the person living on the front lines where the pain is felt and the pills are swallowed.

Healthcare professionals use the art and science of medicine to help patients uncover the truth about what ails them and to help them heal. Like reinforcements meeting up with battle-engaged troops, physicians' initial greetings can bring a measure of relief when all their words and actions communicate the underlying message, "You did a good job to get here. Now let's see what we can do to help."

- We prepare patients to take proper action when we explain the dilemma of knowing when to call or come if symptoms are mild or tolerable.
- We encourage patients to take proper action by acknowledging our dependence on them as part of the team and validating our trust in them.
- We reinforce proper action by complimenting their efforts to call or come in.

Appointment Police

People complain about waiting in physicians' reception rooms for hours on end. But sometimes we are left waiting for patients who never show up. With all we have to do just to keep up, it may seem unreasonable to expect us to go chasing after patients who don't bother to cancel or who cancel at the last minute. But maybe we have a responsibility.

Brngggg. My internist's number lights up on caller-ID and jump-starts my pulse. "Hello?"

"Hi, Wendy. I'm rescheduling all the doctor's appointments. Can you come in next Thursday at 11:30 instead of today?"

"That sounds fine," I reply, struggling to sound nonchalant. "Bye." (*click*)

Flush with relief, I gasp, "My follow-up appointment is today! I would have missed it."

I thank my lucky stars—exactly as my son did two hours earlier when his cell phone displayed the school-generated message, "Classes cancelled due to ice storm."

Memories awaken of times in my internal medicine practice when a patient hadn't shown up. The hassle of shuffling the day's schedule highlighted the opportunity costs of not seeing people on my waiting list. But the harder part was caring for and about these "no-shows." When tracking down truant patients by telephone, my receptionist and medical assistant often resembled mothers whose fretting escalates the longer the clock ticks past curfew. At the moment of contact, professional decorum kept my staff from screaming at the patient, "Thank heavens you're alive; I could kill you for making me worry."

As for the rare repeat offender, our ranting in the privacy of the breakroom ranged from frustration with patients' unreliability to raw fear for patients' well-being. We often debated why each patient missed his or her appointment.

I wonder what they'd say about my near miss. Was it an innocent slip, or do I have the beginnings of Alzheimer's? Would they decide I'm harboring some subconscious need to avoid medical visits?

"I'm so sorry. I guess I forgot." Embarrassed, Ruth scheduled a new follow-up visit. I'm fertilizing this missed-appointment molehill because of Ruth, my cousin. A few months ago Ruth got a call from her doctor's office. "Are you okay, Ruth? You didn't show up for your appointment this morning." Although upset, she took comfort in knowing she'd apologize in person when she went in.

A few weeks later, Ruth happened to glance at her Palm Pilot hours after the appointed time of her rescheduled doctor's visit. As she described it later to me, she literally went numb and burst into uncontrollable tears. A deep sense of shame washed over her, and she felt like she wasn't going to be able to face her doctor again...that she would have to get a new doctor.

For Ruth, the lapse shattered her entire sense of being a thoroughly dependable individual. Until that moment, she'd always thought it odd that people ever needed a reminder call such as those she gets from her dentist's office. The missed appointment became such a crisis for Ruth that she felt the need to find some sense in it.

With the tender loving support of her spouse, Ruth's search for meaning was rewarded when unvoiced fears emerged that explained her uncharacteristic delinquency. Ruth then sent a written apology along with a check that she insisted her doctor cash to cover the missed appointment. Soon after, she received a friendly note: "It happens to the best of our patients. We look forward to seeing you." With a way to save face, Ruth was able to get back on track.

I don't have any appointment-phobia keeping me from follow-ups. To paraphrase a question sent to an advice columnist years ago by a reader who had accidentally typed *Dead Dad* instead of *Dear Dad*, "Must every mistake carry profound Freudian implications?" No, of course not. People are busy. Life is hectic. To err is human. Well-adjusted, well-motivated survivors screw up. And all medical appointments are not the same; clearly some follow-up visits are less important than others.

Normal healthy people miss meetings all the time. But even when all is well, routine medical follow-ups are different from haircut appointments and high-stakes business meetings. After serious illness, just showing up takes courage. Some patients overcome fear of needles. Others brace themselves for pungent memories of sickness, triggered by the deodorizer used in the reception room. And all patients, from high-strung compulsive executives to ditzy teenagers, surmount fear of bad news. At some level, your patients know they wouldn't need the appointment if you already knew they were fine.

A missed appointment is not a problem, but a symptom. For most patients, an isolated incident warrants no more attention than a solitary sneeze. Just as you'd offer a tissue, offer a new appointment. It's when your patient doesn't reschedule or fails to show up a second time that you need to consider underlying physical and/or psychosocial problems.

Does this mean your job description now includes "appointment police"? What if your office doesn't have the time or resources to pursue patients who don't show up? During my residency, an experienced professor once addressed my exasperation regarding a non-compliant patient with an aphorism, "You can't care more about your patients than they do." Decades later, I now see the flaw in his advice: What patients do (or don't do) is not always an accurate reflection of how much they care.

Missed appointments are missed opportunities to heal. The question becomes how best to help patients resume needed follow-up visits. Since a wide variety of complex forces can result in a common outcome—a missed appointment—the answer depends on the specific patient and circumstances.

For some patients (I venture to say most patients), scolding or scaring them only fuels the emotions that are keeping them from returning for follow-ups. Yet for other patients, these tactics are exactly what it takes to get them back into your office. Understanding why your patient missed an appointment helps you to know how to help. Paradoxically, you may need to get the patient in your office to best understand why the patient didn't come to your office.

I'll probably mention my near miss to my doctor when I see her. She can decide either to pursue further evaluation of my memory difficulties or to tell me that such a slip, like my scattered silver-gray hairs, is perfectly normal for a perfectly normal 52-year-old.

I want to get well. Next Thursday, I'll set my cell phone alarm and leave sticky note reminders on my bathroom mirror, breakfast table and computer screen. I'm not taking any chances: the forecast is sunny.

- We are doing our job when we find out why patients miss their appointments.
- We preserve patients' dignity by accepting and validating a single missed appointment as a normal and excusable lapse (if, indeed, it was just a lapse).
- Patients benefit when we explore their repeated lapses as diligently as their other symptoms.

Mantras for Tired Patients

Fatigue is one of the most common complaints heard in our offices, especially from patients who are recovering from serious illness or surgery. Focused on patients with active medical problems, we may feel powerless when patients want relief from fatigue that is part and parcel of their recovery. But we are not.

You pull your next patient's chart off the door and read your nurse's notes, "Last Rx 18 mo ago. C/O persistent fatigue." The patient's scans and blood work are completely normal. In all the other exam rooms, sick patients are waiting. The clock is ticking.

How can you help these patients in remission who are doing relatively well? Let's assume you've already addressed all treatable causes of your patients' fatigue and have advised them on diet and exercise. Clearly if they get tired, they should do less. But living within limits is not that easy, as I learned only after I developed persistent post-cancer fatigue.

I was just a kid when I appreciated the existential problem of limits. Looking at a picture book one day, I mused: "If the cows on the farm never venture near the perimeter barbed wire, they never know they are fenced in." It is my earliest recollection of the realization that perception shapes reality. Decades later, as I struggled with fatigue, this valuable insight for survivors was lost on me.

As a physician, I'd spent years advising patients about recognizing and respecting their physical limits while, at the same time, ignoring my own. My medical training had ingrained that the only acceptable response to call-related fatigue was sucking it up, focusing harder, drinking a cup or two of strong coffee and soldiering on.

This ethos of holding up my end was reinforced on a regular basis. I remember waiting for an elevator and watching a colleague lean against the wall, diaphoretic and coughing. When I asked if he was okay, he responded, "Yeah. Pneumonia. But I'm on antibiotics, so I'm not putting any patients at risk." My maternal instincts kicked in and I asked if, maybe, he needed to go home. "No, no. It's *walking* pneumonia."

When I first became a patient, soldiering on wasn't an option. With growth stimulating factors and effective nausea medications still a year shy of FDA approval, I was forced to take a leave of absence for the duration of my myelo-ramming chemotherapy.

My fatigue problem began once treatment ended. I'd assured everyone that as soon as my counts recovered I'd resume the mantle of patient care. But my expectations proved overly optimistic, especially after undergoing additional courses of treatment.

Of all the challenges of my early remissions, the invisible wound of fatigue was the biggest bugaboo. I kept misjudging and then reneging on commitments or getting stuck at the grocery store with a full wagon and too little energy to drive home. I was constantly apologizing to loved ones for creating problems due to my fatigue-hampered judgment, memory or performance. For all my achievements, my adjustment to the fatigue aspect of my "new normal" was a disaster. Like a BMW with a half-gallon fuel tank, I functioned well only for a short while before running out of gas.

My first task was learning to recognize my energy limits. Of course, my doctors couldn't send off a red top for a "fatigue level" along with a CBC. Drugstores didn't sell fatigue-o-meters alongside the sphygmomanometers to help me monitor my energy level at home. And when I got tired, my nose didn't turn purple, so my friends and loved ones couldn't really help me out. Over time, I learned to recognize not only tiredness, but also word block, headaches and irritability as signals of waning energy.

More challenging was respecting my limits. Even after I figured out how much I could and couldn't do under this circumstance or that, I resisted slowing down or resting, but for different reasons than when I was working as a physician.

With much of my life feeling out of control, a stupid cut-off-my-nose-to-spite-my-face stubbornness led me to try to hold on to the sense of control that accompanies not giving in to fatigue. I delayed naps because lying down stirred up residual grief by adding whatever activities I was missing to my many cancer-related losses. The list of explanations uncovered through counseling goes on and on. Living in a 24/7 society that undervalues sleep didn't help either.

The essential truth is that when I respect my limits, I feel well. The irony is that feeling well triggers thoughts and feelings that sabotage respecting my limits. "Hmm, I feel good. Maybe I don't need to limit myself anymore."

Even when I keep in mind that I'm fine *because* I'm respecting my limits, kindly comments from friends and family take their toll. "You look great. So healthy! Do you think you'll return to patient care?"

For patients who struggle with fatigue, counseling can help them tease apart the underlying psychodynamics. But for some patients, just giving them a handout with some mantras may do the trick:

Mantra #1: "It's good to feel good, so do what you need to do to feel good."

Mantra #2: "Sleeping is not wasting time."

Mantra #3: "Pushing your limits is like rubbing up against a barbed wire fence: you can keep going, but it's painful, exhausting, unhealthy and not pretty."

Mantra #4: "While respecting current limits, you can still hope for improvement. Nourish that hope by taking steps to increase your fitness and overall health."

Mantra #5: "Test your limits occasionally—not every day!—to see if the measures you're taking and the passage of time have made a difference. But once re-evaluated, resume respecting your current limits, whatever they are."

If nothing else, you can share with your patients what I learned from the cows on the farm: "Respecting your limits can set you free."

- We comfort patients by explaining that illness-related fatigue is different than the normal fatigue that healthy people feel at the end of a long day.
- We reassure patients by periodically screening for all treatable causes of fatigue.
- We help tired patients take proper action by advising them on energy-conserving measures.

Visualizing the Buzz

When patients asked my opinion regarding visualization as a complementary therapy, I felt obligated to respond honestly. If I were practicing medicine today, I'd give a different answer than I gave years ago.

My professor's trick was as old as the hills. He instructed, "Imagine slicing through a lemon. Bring the cut surface to your lips and inhale the citrus aroma. Now imagine biting down and sucking the sour juices." With my parotids pulsating, his lesson was ingrained forever: The mind affects the body.

Beginning in those freshman days of medical school, I thought about the mind-body connection while learning how to evaluate and treat patients. By the time I opened my internal medicine practice, I routinely addressed the emotions causing or exacerbating my patients' symptoms, instead of dismissing them with a diagnosis of "psychosomatic." And I wasn't the only one paying attention to the mind-body connection.

In the mid-1980s a revolution was reverberating in cancer survivor communities. Self-help books trumpeted the untapped healing power of the mind. Like Professor Hill in *The Music Man*—the con man who instructed kids to "Think the Minuet in G"—mega-selling authors were convincing patients to "Visualize your immune system destroying your cancer cells."

I scoffed. Sure, I occasionally prescribed biofeedback or counseling for my tensed-up patients who could benefit from visualization techniques. But ridding the body of cancer cells is as different from relaxing muscles as regenerating a new limb is different from repairing a paper cut.

My stance was unshaken after my own cancer diagnosis. Throughout my chemotherapy, the only visualizing I did was that of my patients' records leaving my office and my future disappearing. I had better uses for my time and energy than conjuring images of chemo-assisted healthy leukocytes ambushing my lymphoma cells.

Only 19 months after beginning my first course of treatment, I began a second course, this time minimantle for a local recurrence. Like a damsel tied to train tracks, I was frightened by the threat of advancing cancer and worried about radiation's long-term risks. But with regard to my imminent first radiation session, I had no concerns. Radiation would feel like having my photograph taken. Right?

Not always. The technician immobilized my head and neck in a custom-made mask tethered to the table. Then she left the room. The thick door closed. *Click.* A square of light radiated onto me from the linear accelerator's overhanging gantry, accompanied by a strangely familiar buzz. After 30 seconds or so, the skin of my neck got warm. I thought, "Hey, what's this? I'm not supposed to feel anything." So I focused. "Yes, my skin is definitely warm. And getting warmer."

The treatment ended. On my way out of the Rad-Onc department, I saw my radiation oncologist. "How'd it go?" he asked.

"Fine, but I was shocked my skin got warm. I expected to feel nothing."

His response was immediate and matter-of-fact: "Your skin wasn't warm, Wendy. You just imagined it because you were scared."

I walked away thinking, "What? Imagined it? Whew, they hadn't goofed and zapped me with too much radiation! But I imagined that? No way. That warmth was real."

Over the next few hours, my unconscious search for the fodder feeding my supposed fear turned up a variety of images. Hiding under my desk in elementary school during nuclear air raid drills. Feeling the weight of the lead apron on my budding breasts while listening to the distinctive buzz of my dentist's Panorex camera. Extra-carefully handling radioactive tracers while doing receptor research as an undergrad. And most recently, hurrying out of the room after comforting one of my patients as she was positioned for emergency x-rays.

"Hmm. Could I have a long-standing fear of radiation expressing itself in physical symptoms during chosen exposure to high-dose radiation?"

The next day, the technicians strapped me down and the door clicked closed. Once again, I watched the square of light and listened to the buzz. And I waited, wondering what I would feel. After 30 seconds, nothing happened. Before I knew it, the buzz stopped. Still nothing.

I was amazed, not that my fear had caused physical symptoms the day before, but that I'd undervalued the power of my mind and had been thumbing my nose at an opportunity to channel it toward my healing. If my mind could make me feel warmth, then my mind could help me feel hungry after chemo and help me diminish my leg pain. For the rest of my sessions, I responded to the buzz by visualizing the x-rays killing my lymphoma cells.

My dramatic mind-body experience opened my eyes to the broad range of people who can benefit from visualization, not just the occasional patient with extreme anxiety-induced symptoms. And it highlighted a danger: Patients experiencing the ability of the mind to relieve psychosomatic symptoms can too easily make the leap to believing their mind has the power to heal their cancer. In extreme cases, patients may abandon conventional or investigational therapies.

So what role does visualization play in determining outcome? Moviegoers hungry for a happy ending to *The Music Man* are tempted to buy into Hill's "Think Method," especially when the footage behind the credits shows Hill's students transformed into a professional marching band.

But before the credits begin, the official end of the story broadcasts a message for survivors who measure success by the results. After months of using the Think Method, the kids play the Minuet in G. Their performance stirs genuine pride and joy, but those kids couldn't play in tune if their lives depended on it.

Did my visualization help kill my cancer cells? No, the radiation did that. But visualizing did calm me and nourish my hope by transforming radiation from a source of fear to one of confidence.

Researchers today are exploring scientifically how the mind affects the body, such as how stress depresses the immune system. In the meantime, many patients who are feeling stressed—and trust me, illness is stressful—are also feeling pressure from books and well-wishers to think themselves well. Sadly, for those whose illness progresses despite concerted efforts to visualize, many feel guilty or ashamed that they failed to control their disease.

Healthcare professionals can relieve these unnecessary burdens by explaining that we have no objective evidence that visualization kills cancer cells or restores myelin or replaces irreversibly damaged heart muscle. But it does help patients—psychologically and emotionally—get through effective treatments. Whether by bringing comfort or improving compliance, guided imagery can help patients use the power of the mind in healing ways.

- We help patients by supporting their use of visualization as a complementary therapy, only if we also clarify the limits of this modality.
- We help patients by pointing out that visualization calms some patients and increases anxiety for others.
- For anxious patients who can benefit, referral for counseling and visualization enhances compliance by increasing their sense of control.

"Killer" Coke

Most medical school curricula include relatively little about nutrition. Yet diet is one factor in healing under patients' total control. And the reality is that a variety of people who are not trained in nutritional sciences influence patients' food choices.

Ms. Redhead isn't the first person to shoot me a look of disdain. She enters the foyer all perky and neatly coiffed, and then ambles over to my book-signing table. Her friendly smile doesn't fool me one bit as her gaze flits from my hair to my necklace to my hands.

"Are you Wendy?" she asks, as if searching for Waldo in a crowd.

I nod slowly, acutely aware that survivorship events offer fertile ground for selling hopeful wares. Ms. Redhead lingers at my table, not to buy a book but to size up my beliefs. How do I know? It doesn't take a Sherlock, given the brand name emblazoned in bold letters on her shirt.

"Hi," she says.

"Hello," I answer.

Her toothy smile puts me on guard. As expected, she asks if I'm familiar with the nutritional supplement she sells.

"Yes," I answer, knowing what's coming next.

"Do you take it?"

The little shake of my head is more than enough to launch her scientific-studies-filled spiel. Mid-sentence, she stumbles, tripped up by her sudden discovery.

Uh oh. I blanch and want to hide. She found me out. I squirm. I blush. You would think the tip of my drinking straw is dipping into a petite peak of white powder, not a red aluminum can encircled with a wavy white stripe.

C-C-Coke?" she asks, practically choking on the word. Leaning in closer, she whispers, "Yours?"

I nod sheepishly, imagining the gears churning in her head: "Cross Wendy's books off my list of recommended readings."

After what feels like forever, Ms. Redhead straightens up, still waiting for my answer. I look at my can of Coke, off to the side of the book-signing table. Then I look back at my accuser and realize it is totally silly for me to be ashamed of indulging in an occasional carbonated sugar-and-caffeine fix.

Don't get me wrong: Healthful diet is a vital element in healing and good health. I absolutely believe that. Hey, I was a vegetarian for many years and, since high school days, have always watched what I eat. But let's be realistic. My body has reserves. If I want a buzz before giving a talk, drinking half a can of Coke every once in a while isn't going to kill me.

Reaching for my red can, I think of all the things I could say. I slowly pull out the straw and place it neatly on a nearby napkin. Then I push the can toward Ms. Redhead, "Would you like some? It's a nice treat on occasion." Ms. Redhead sighs and walks away. I take another sip. No sale.

***

Researchers are sorting out scientifically what foods and supplements might put the brakes on malignant cells. Meanwhile, vendors to the vulnerable are dispensing what doctor's can't: a sense of certainty. Their winsome expressions radiate wholesomeness: "I care about you and just want you to get well. I'd like to share information that can help."

Cynics point out that such caring and sharing puts money in peddlers' pockets. For argument's sake, let's assume these people are motivated by pure altruism and don't make a penny. And let's focus solely on the problem of unsolicited advice about diet.

Patients seem to be held to a higher dietary standard. People who believe—or want to believe—in the curative power of certain foods pass harsh judgments on patients who eat red meat, munch a bunch of Fritos or drink soda.

Here's the problem: Patients want to get well. Living with uncertainty, they submit to harsh treatments month after month, sometimes year after year. In contrast to all the factors in healing beyond their control, what patients put in their mouths is theirs to decide. Consequently, many patients wonder or worry if they are choosing wisely. This, together with the fact that everyone eats, opening the door for everyone—from Registered Dieticians to Ms. Redheads—to have strong opinions and pass judgments on patients' food choices.

The link between eating and healing is complex. So our obligation goes beyond instructing our patients about specific contraindications and offering dietary guidelines or referring patients to nutritionists. Along with encouraging patients' efforts to eat healthful diets, we must warn them about the Ms. Redheads.

Relieve patients of the burdens of unnecessary deprivation and underserved guilt by making it clear that they don't have to do everything perfectly. Even when a particular diet is known to help survival, healing has room for slippage. Patients shouldn't be afraid of

"Killer" Coke. As long as what patients do is safe, it's okay to live a little. When surviving cancer or other illness, isn't that the point?

- We encourage patients to take proper action by explaining how diet is one factor in healing that is totally under their control.
- We empower patients by guiding them toward personalized healthful diets.
- We relieve a burden by reassuring them their diets don't have to be perfect.

Cancer Sticks

You would think that after suffering an MI or undergoing chemotherapy for lung cancer, patients would be motivated to quit smoking forever. After we've done our best to get patients through smoking-related illnesses, learning that patients have taken up cigarettes again can stir intense emotions.

Every time Sally came in for her checkup, my receptionist, Judy, perked up. My medical assistant, Kathy, presented Sally's chart to me with a flourish instead of just leaving it in the plastic holder on the exam room door. Success stories such as Sally's broke the drudgery and disappointment of treating smokers who were sick with horrid diseases.

Gratitude prompted our star patient to hug anyone who had ever injected, positioned, biopsied or otherwise participated in her complication-strewn road to recovery. We happily complied. Touching our walking-talking miracle of modern medicine recharged our batteries to "Full."

Just days before her only daughter's wedding, Sally had been diagnosed with cancer and given a dismal prognosis. Our feisty patient swore off cigarettes cold turkey and arrived early for every test and treatment.

Although she missed her daughter's wedding, she had no regrets. We puffed out our chests while sweet-smelling Sally reveled in her remission. Last week, we heard Sally had become a grandmother.

I am just back from my hospital rounds when I see Kathy slip Sally's chart in the rack and walk off. The vein on the side of Kathy's temple is pulsating prominently like a hazard warning.

I glance at Kathy's notes and enter the exam room, relieved by the healthy vital signs that match my grinning granny.

"Oh good, you brought me pictures!" Leaning over to ooh and aah, I gasp. The mint-and-smoke smell knocks me off-balance.

In the break room three hours later Kathy can't let it go. "How could she?" It is more an accusation than a question.

"Kathy, it's not your fault—or mine," I say calmly. "This is America. As long as I'm certain our patients understand the risks, they get to choose how they live, and they can trust I'll take care of them."

"Dr. Harpham, look at…." Kathy rattles off the names of patients suffering from diseases devoid of modifiable risk factors. "These people would do anything to stay healthy."

"She's addicted, Kathy. Part of her brain lets her believe cancer won't happen to her."

Kathy is shaking her head, "She calls cigarettes 'cancer sticks.' She almost *died* of cancer. Sally can't possibly be in denial."

"What can I say?" I shrug, "Nicotine makes smart people do stupid things."

When Sally stopped smoking, I just assumed the cancer diagnosis had frightened her enough to quit forever. Throughout the months of treatment, it might have been the terrible chemo-taste or maybe it was the overwhelming guilt about burdening her family that kept Sally from lighting up.

Then, as commonly happens after survivors venture forth, the further Sally got from treatment, the weaker her resolve must have become. And one day, the urge to smoke won out—an urge that many smokers say never ever goes away.

While Kathy microwaves her coffee, I start thinking about the hours I spent talking with Sally and her family. On more than one occasion, I deliberately but delicately laid crepe while also nourishing the trickle of hope. When Sally completed treatment, our hope grew. Now, all over again, I fear for her survival.

Suddenly I'm fuming, envisioning Sally's reaction if I were to lick the needle before inserting it into her vein. We are supposed to be a team. How can Sally expect us to be unfailingly diligent and compassionate while she's sabotaging her recovery?

I start thinking about medical situations where my patients might behave "badly"—say, by falling out of bed or by pulling out their NG or ET tube, and I don't hesitate to order and enforce precautionary measures. Guardrails. Sedatives. Wrist restraints. But Sally is not delirious or demented.

Kathy interrupts my thoughts, "Dr. Harpham, what did you say to Sally?"

As with all my smokers, I treaded lightly, not wanting to threaten her autonomy or trust by embarrassing or humiliating her or by sounding like I'm blaming her for her misfortune. "I didn't know what to say, Kathy. So I acted as if I didn't notice."

My assistant storms out, her frustration and anger polluting the air. All alone, I feel defeated and helpless.

**

A whiff of tobacco on the breath of patients can elicit a sticky wicket of feelings and ethical questions among their doctors and nurses.

In retrospect, my satisfaction with informed decision-making let me off the hook too easily. As a patient, I've experienced how knowing the right thing to do can be a far cry from doing it. We often need help.

Patients who resume smoking aren't trying to sabotage their recovery. Nicotine withdrawal triggers physiologic changes in the brain that prompt many patients to make poor choices. Some patients really miss all the pleasures of lighting up. Some claim the nicotine counteracts their fatigue and helps them feel mentally clearer. And, irony of ironies, some patients smoke to regain a sense of control over *something* or to calm the anxiety caused by fear of their disease flaring up again.

For physicians and nurses, smoking as a problem is not nearly as glamorous as neutropenic fever or papilledema. And effective cessation programs that combine medication and psychotherapy are decidedly low-tech, where they even exist.

But we are supposed to be a team. Granted, our best efforts won't always succeed. If patients don't really want to quit smoking or other unhealthy habits, or if patients aren't willing to put forth the effort and make the sacrifices, we can't do it for them. But, that doesn't mean we shouldn't try.

A diagnosis of serious illness creates a teachable moment for smokers, empowering many to finally quit. At the end of cancer treatment, we should address the risk of smoking relapse with the same diligence we address the risk of disease recurrence. Doing so might be more healing for everyone.

- We lose an opportunity to help if we ignore evidence of smoking.
- We help patients take proper action by addressing their addiction with the same diligence we address health risks that are unrelated to behavior.
- We motivate proper action by referring them to resources that can help.

Sugar Pills

When patients demand therapies that can only help by virtue of their placebo effect, the temptation to go ahead and prescribe them may be great.

Lunch couldn't be livelier, with the conversation flitting like a butterfly from topic to topic. Jenny lifts the lid on the white ceramic bowl. "Look, little brother: sugar cubes. Remember how Grandpa used to put one between his front teeth and drink his tea through it?"

"Sure," Ben says, plopping three cubes into his steaming expresso. "Hey, 'sugar' reminds me: Did you read in today's paper that half of American doctors routinely prescribe placebos?"

"It was old news to me," Jenny says, maneuvering two sugar cubes with tongs.

"The article shocked me out of my shoes," Ben said. "Had you heard of obecalp before?"

"Placebo backwards," Jenny chuckles, amused by her younger brother. "Brilliant, eh? The mom who patented it knew she could bypass the FDA."

"Jen, can you imagine your internist prescribing a placebo?"

"Sure. Placebos work," she responds.

Ben lowers his fork and raises his voice, "But it's unethical."

"You didn't worry about ethics last week when I brought you some 'Jewish penicillin.' And my matzo ball soup cured your sniffles, didn't it?" Jenny smiles lovingly.

Ben's voice tightens, "Hey, I'm serious."

"Okay, okay," Jenny says quickly. "As I see it, placebos offer a safe and effective way to help patients. Especially when their problems are all in the head or are due to a medical condition with no good treatment options, what's wrong with trying placebos?"

"What happens if patients Google their meds and discover they were given dummy pills?"

Jenny quips, "They should appreciate getting better and be glad they didn't go through a slew of expensive tests."

"Then how could they trust their doctors again, after doling out good money for sugar pills?"

Jenny pokes Ben's arm, "That's the point. They do trust their doctors, because their doctors always use the best therapy for the situation. And some situations call for placebos."

"If it were me and I got sick again, I'd wonder if I should even fill my prescription."

"Maybe that's because you're a cancer survivor, Ben. The average patient doesn't get as involved in their care."

Ben leans forward, "Sure they do." He leans back again. "You know, I thought a lot about placebos when I was in the trial to prevent CMV after my transplant, and…"

"Wait. Doesn't that confirm your belief in the use of placebos? You signed a consent form agreeing to the possibility of receiving a placebo."

"Thanks for bolstering my argument, Sis: I *knew* I might get a placebo. Placebos were not given to help me get better; they were given to help determine the effect of the trial drug. Nobody was trying to fool me. Even the researchers didn't know if I was getting a drug or placebo."

"True." Jenny concedes, realizing that until this moment she'd always lumped together all placebos.

"Meanwhile," Ben says emphatically, "practitioners know exactly what they are prescribing, purposely trying to trick the patient into feeling better."

Sobered by her brother's insight, she stands by her conviction that placebos have a place in practice. "So are you saying moms shouldn't put band-aids on their kids' bruises anymore, since the plastic strips make the pain go away purely through their effect on expectations and emotions?"

"Jenny, we're talking about professionals prescribing placebos, not moms kissing boo-boos. In doctor-patient relationships, the ends don't justify the means."

"Haven't you heard the saying, 'Cure sometimes, relieve often, comfort always,' li'l brother? You've seen Mom reach for her pills and feel better before they even reach her stomach."

"Jen, I'm just saying that placebos damage the sacred bond of trust. Why can't Mom's physicians elicit the exact same effect with words of encouragement—or, maybe, counseling or something like physical therapy—instead of sugar pills?"

"Because in our culture medicines are uniquely powerful potions," Jenny insists. "We'd only be hurting ourselves if we outlawed placebos."

Ben senses an impasse. "Let's call it a draw on sugar pills."

***

Do placebos have a legitimate place in the proverbial black bags of competent and compassionate physicians? Or is the damage to doctor-patient relationships too great to ever justify "royal lies"?

Any useful discussion of placebos that takes place in a white tower of academic medicine must include practicing clinicians from the front lines of patient care. Patients often demand, for example, antibiotics to treat viral illnesses or another round of chemo that is highly unlikely to help in any way. Time-pressured physicians may relent, scribbling a 'script for antibiotics instead of taking the time to once again explain the risks of side effects and colonization with resistant bugs, not to mention the global problem of antibiotic resistance. And oncologists, in their efforts not to extinguish patients' hope—or to avoid discussing hospice—might justify prescribing another round of ineffective treatment. As a physician-survivor, I appreciate both sides and remain troubled by the use of placebos in practice.

Seismic shifts in modern doctor-patient relationships demand a closer look at the use of placebos. I hope the wrangling doesn't distract us from a more useful quest: exploring how to tap into the power to heal now harnessed by placebos, only without any element of deception.

Therapeutic modalities built on trust build on the strengths of science and compassion and avoid the ethical concerns raised by placebos. I envision a future when trust remains an inviolable element of healing physician-patient relationships and placebos are relegated to history books.

- We build the trust that helps patients take proper action by distinguishing placebos used in clinical trials from placebos used in clinical practice.
- We enhance the benefit of proven therapies by harnessing the healing power of expectation and hope.

CHAPTER 4

Meaning

"We are here to add what we can to life, not to get what we can from life."

Sir William Osler

My cancer diagnosis disrupted everything I knew as normal and launched me on a spiritual journey. Like millions of other patients with serious or chronic illness, I questioned who I was and searched for understanding about my life's purpose.

The people you'd expect to support me on this personal quest were, indeed, the major players: my husband, my closest friends, my rabbi, and the oncology social worker. Years later (and only in retrospect), I realized how much my physicians and nurses had helped me, too.

The following stories revolve around the theme of meaning. This is perhaps the most challenging chapter because "meaning" signifies something different to everyone. Even if you were a philosophy or theology major before embarking on your medical career, you might feel these questions are too big or too personal to address in the clinical setting. As it is, you barely have time to tend to patients' medical concerns. "Besides," you might point out to me, "not all patients are interested in exploring existential issues."

I agree. I've known patients who, except for showing up for their appointments and treatments, don't pay attention to their illness. These patients erect a psychic barrier around their trauma, like a plaster cast encasing a fractured limb. If their treatment ordeal has an ending, they then turn their back on this period of their life, never to talk of it again.

But many patients—including me—do explore the metaphysical questions of life. Most have little choice: The pain and loss associated with life-altering illness thrust "meaning" center stage. We patients feel compelled to figure out who we are and what we believe. And truth be told, I still worry about those patients who approach their illness Rambo-style, trying to ignore obvious pain and loss. As you'll see from these stories, rare is the individual whose sense of self is not rocked, at least a little, by illness or injury.

I've come to believe that clinicians can't afford to cordon off philosophical and spiritual issues when addressing their patients' medical concerns. Whether or not you want to or mean to, your words and actions can affect your patients' sense of self and sense of meaning in their lives, often in profound ways.

Don't worry: I have no intention of delving deeply. In keeping with the title of this book, my goals are modest. I hope only to scratch the surface of the age-old questions, so we can help patients as they wrestle with concerns about "meaning."

This chapter begins with a reflection on empathy. You'll see how for years I didn't acknowledge my oncologist's empathy, even as his expressions of concern were helping me heal. This is a particularly sensitive story for me to share, because if any characteristic helps define our humanity it is our empathy. This ability to imagine and identify with the thoughts and feelings of another person explains why physicians can never be replaced by machines. Empathy is why medicine has always been—and will always be—about people caring for people.

Then I switch gears, telling a tongue-in-cheek true story of my first minivan, named Blueberry, to highlight a serious insight about the human condition. This is intended as a fun way to talk about giving patients a little latitude when they are terse with you or your staff.

For the next three stories, I hunker down with some big questions: What does it mean to succeed or fail? What does it mean to find and fulfill one's life purpose? I illustrate how, with the power of a few words or by looking in a patient's eyes, clinicians can guide a patient toward or away from a healthy sense of self and purpose.

Then I shift the focus to the innocent bystanders in many illness dramas: the normal, healthy children of patients with serious or chronic illness. "Conversation 2008" is a mock interview with my three kids, giving voice to their message to physicians and nurses: "Please help our parents hold on to their identity as parents."

Bringing this chapter to a close, I look at final good-byes between clinicians and patients, a poignant moment when what you say—or don't say—can solidify or shatter a healing clinician-patient relationship.

These are tough topics. That's okay. The more we think and talk about them, the more likely we are to see opportunities for healing.

Empathy

Sir Frances Peabody's famous 1927 quote serves as a guiding mantra for clinicians: "The secret of the care of the patient is in caring for the patient." In my practice, I assumed my patients appreciated when I was empathetic. But maybe sometimes they couldn't.

"When it comes to medical care, empathy is over-rated."

At least that's what I thought when I was first diagnosed. All I wanted was an oncologist who was brilliant, experienced, knowledgeable and up-to-date. He or she had to be objective, cool under pressure, high-energy and responsive, too. Oh, and not too busy to see me quickly. Was that asking too much?

I didn't think so, since that's what I wanted for the patients I sent to surgeons or whatever-ologists. My referral spiel often emphasized the importance of expertise and technical skill over hand-holding.

"If it were me," I'd tell my patients as I wrote down consultants' names and numbers, "I wouldn't care if they seemed cold, as long as when they're cutting on me (or prescribing chemo or 'scoping me) they are the best at what they do."

I'd then put my hand on my patient's knee or forearm reassuringly. "Your family and I can provide all the comfort and support you need."

Meanwhile, my own professional style was based on old-fashioned caring while delivering high-tech medicine. I valued the power of empathetic words to shape my patients' perceptions and responses positively, calm their anxiety and nourish their hope.

This double-standard—striving to deliver compassionate care to my patients while downplaying empathy as a priority when choosing my own oncologist—didn't faze me. As a patient, I had plenty of people feeling my pain: My husband adored me and always put my needs before his. My friends and family were in the wings, waiting for marching orders. I thought that knowing my oncologist was fully immersed in conquering my cancer cells would comfort me more than his or her empathy. So when my internist suggested consulting Dr. S., I readily agreed.

This oncologist—nicknamed "the walking encyclopedia" by the house staff—was even-tempered and hardworking. On numerous occasions, he'd blown me away by asking penetrating questions or offering astute diagnoses outside his field of expertise. His ever-enthusiastic recounting of clinical studies convinced me this man couldn't get enough of the science of medicine.

Friends and family would occasionally ask if my doctor was nice. "Sure. (I guess.)" I didn't pay much attention, because Dr. S. was my point man for objective medical issues. When it came to emotions, I turned to the nurses to mop up my tears and shore up my courage as I grieved and adjusted to the tsunami of unwanted changes.

Two or so years after my diagnosis, I was talking with Dr. S.'s nurse, professional-to-professional. In the context of sharing insights that might be useful in her care of other patients, I described the difficulty of facing recurrence and closing my medical practice. She mentioned, "Dr. S. was sad you were so sad."

I was stunned—and speechless. Until that moment, I'd never entertained a moment's thought about the effect of my illness on Dr. S. I thought, "I'm just like my patients who asked my receptionist, 'Whose baby is this?' while pointing to the picture of a newborn infant on the check-in counter." My receptionist had answered, "Dr. Harpham's, of course."

My staff couldn't believe how many patients hadn't noticed the buttons straining to keep my white coat closed at their prior visits—even just weeks before I gave birth. But they had been too focused on their problems to notice.

Most of what little I remember from the first year of my illness is blurry. Yet when I concentrate, a few sharp memories tell volumes. Dr. S. chose his words wisely, for example describing my indolent lymphoma as "very treatable" when at my first office visit I asked rhetorically, "My cancer is curable, right?" Whenever my emotions made it difficult for me to respond quickly he patiently gave me whatever time I needed. And he often swung by the infusion room on my chemo days just to say, "Hi."

Had I been a third party to our interactions, undoubtedly I would have recognized and acknowledged Dr. S.'s empathy. But for a long time, I'd been too sick, scared and, like my patients, self-absorbed for any of it to register.

That is not to say his caring didn't make a difference for me. It did. As a patient, I was like a starving toddler who accepts needed food from a concerned adult. Although thankful to have my pain relieved and to be nourished in ways that helped me grow, I didn't recognize or express gratitude for the compassion behind the responses that helped me heal.

The discipline of medicine demands mastery of the science and technology of medical care. But this noble calling also requires an ability to understand patients' situations, feelings and motives, and to respond with compassion. Throughout the early years of my illness, my awareness of and gratitude for the gift of my physician's empathy were dulled by my fear, pain and adaptive self-centeredness. Had I not been in the position of talking collegially with his nurse that day, I don't know how long it would have taken me to thank Dr. S.

My perspective from both sides of the stethoscope helps me appreciate the value of empathy in medicine. I can now tell you this wholeheartedly: Empathy matters.

Some patients get well and move on before becoming conscious of and grateful for your compassion. Others die without ever breaking through the fog of self-absorption. Consequently, patients may never thank you for your expressions of empathy that help them live.

I trust I am speaking for other patients when I say, "Thanks for caring."

- Empathy does matter.
- We can take comfort in knowing that our empathy helps our patients even when they are too sick, scared and self-absorbed to notice it.
- We can take comfort in knowing that most patients feel grateful for our empathy without ever acknowledging it.

Blueberry

Some days speed bumps slow you down every which way you turn. Anything from a misfiled lab report to a patient fainting in one of your exam rooms can put a crimp in your day. You might expect your patients to understand that you and your staff are doing your best. So your feathers might get ruffled by a patient who gets snippy with your staff (or with you) because a test result still isn't ready or you are running behind schedule.

With love and affection I am naming her Blueberry. The "new" smell makes me swoon as my fingers slide over the slick cup holders and regionally controlled air vents. Time will tell if the preceding weeks of car-dealership shopping and checking out *Consumer Reports®* paid off. Along with safety features and budget constraints, I care about reliability, a top priority since I'm in cancer treatment and can't afford a breakdown.

A week or so into my blue-minivan bliss, the sky opens up. I turn on the wipers. The wipers don't turn on. "What the…?" Leaning forward—as if with my face touching the windshield I could peek between the raindrops for a clear view of the road—I make a U-turn and head straight to the dealership, all the while muttering to myself, "No big deal. Just a minor new-car wrinkle." After not one, not two, but three visits to the dealership, Blueberry is cured of misfiring wipers.

A few weeks go by before I notice a weird buzzing noise coming from the dash. I'd like to turn the radio louder and forget about it, but I do the right thing and take Blueberry to the shop. Two days later my mechanic has the problem diagnosed and fixed, and I'm back behind the wheel. It takes another day or two before I assume I'll get to where I'm going, instead of listening for the buzz and wondering if my beloved blue minivan can make the trip without a hitch.

Blueberry reminds me of my recurrent cancer. I'd rather be writing or speaking or doing pretty much anything—even laundry—instead of going to the cancer clinic (again) for more diagnostic scans, consultations, treatments, and post-treatment exams. I've long ago accepted that life is unfair and you gotta do what you gotta do, but—and I'm not complaining, just stating facts—cancer can be so darned inconvenient when I'm trying to live my life. Her Royal Highness signals me with an enlarged lymph node here or a new pain there, and I have to drop what I'm doing and respond to her demands (maybe not that minute or even that day, but soon enough).

"What now?" My kids are howling with delight at Blueberry's latest antics. The inside lights are blinking on and off. I see my afternoon plans vaporize. Then a warning *Ding-ding-ding* sounds in rhythm with the flashing lights. I shift gears and pay attention to everything, so I can give a good history to my buddy at the dealership who now recognizes my voice from "Hello." I'm not the least bit worried. He'll find the electrical glitch and get it fixed. Eventually, anyway.

He's fixing Blueberry while I'm getting a lift home and while I'm taking my husband to work (so I can borrow hubby's reliable 11-year old car). He's still fixing Blueberry while I'm picking up my husband from work and, later, when I'm stuck at home while my daughter drives to practice. Finally, he calls to tell me Blueberry is "like new." Like new? Like "Blueberry new"? Or like "good car new"? So I find someone to drop me off at the dealership, where I wait in line to pay and then wait for them to bring her out. Buckled up, I drive back home, watching and waiting to see if the current problem is really fixed.

Everyone has car troubles now and then, but Blueberry is a lemon. She may not meet the legal criteria under the Lemon Law since each new problem is repaired in three or less visits. But hey, a rose is a rose.

Dang! The ignition won't turn. I'm calling a tow truck. I'm canceling my plans so that I can take Blueberry to the dealership for her thirty-sixth (and counting) service visit. Ah, my poor One-and-only with the cool cup holders and regionally controlled air vents. My sweet Blueberry. I must hold onto hope that this repair is my last repair and the end of my car troubles.

Hallelujah! Now six years later, I can tell you it was.

***

A million reasons can explain why patients get edgy or rude or demanding. They may be in pain, sleep-deprived, frightened, or angry at the whole world. Or, in fact, they may be feeling pretty good, totally at peace with their disease and their Maker, and most grateful for their healthcare team, but they are momentarily torqued by the inconvenience of their illness.

I try to deal in healthy ways with both my cancer and my car. After linking up with qualified professionals, I comply with their prescriptions and am punctual with tune-ups. When early signs of trouble develop or serial problems wear me out, I strive for the equanimity needed to do the right thing. I even try making lemonade out of lemons, blending optimism and humor with hope. Yet when feeling trapped by fate, I occasionally break down, leaking expressions of frustration and anger. I am so, so sorry.

I've learned that whether dealing with cancer or a problem-prone car, it helps to go with the flow. But illness is different than car troubles (or most anything else, for that matter). Patients who feel pushed to the breaking point don't have the option of trade-ins or trade-ups, only trade-offs. This is a reality of which I am reminded every time I leave the cancer clinic and confidently buckle up in Greenbean, my reliable green van.

- Patients deserve a little latitude if they act impatient on occasion.
- Giving patients as much control as possible lessens their sense of being trapped.
- We help patients heal when we acknowledge their patience and fortitude.

A Meeting with Failure

At a luncheon years ago, a prominent oncologist seated next to me described his sense of failure because a longtime patient died. I respectfully asked why that meant he failed. His answer was unsettling, but I felt I couldn't push the discussion in that setting.

"I failed my patient." Greg's surrender is resolute as he leans to his left. A waiter slips a glass of ice water in front of this passionate physician whose eyes reflect sorrow for his patient.

"You failed?" This question suggests concern about a misguided treatment decision or misspoken word.

"She died," Greg responds.

Ever the caregiver, he asks a rhetorical question, hoping it will stop the grieving doctor from beating up on himself. "Hey, Doc, did your patient get good care?"

Greg responds by reviewing his state-of-the art approach, carefully recounting the initial treatments as if he were reading his patient's opened chart, not his lunch menu.

"And then? A trial?" This question refers not to malpractice proceedings but to clinical trials that offer promising treatments in research settings.

"Two Phase II and one Phase I," Greg says. But her cancer, like her hope, was tenacious." Setting down his menu to scan the roomful of diners, as if more than just he should buck up and stand accountable, Greg adds, "We all failed her."

"We? Who?"

"Clinicians, researchers, all of us. We call ourselves healers? We failed her, her children, her husband." Greg's disappointment and disgust are as real as a teenager's despair over a nose too big or breasts too small.

"You say, 'We failed.' How did we fail?"

"She had the best treatment anyone could offer, and it wasn't enough!" A fleeting look of exasperation and an upturned palm punctuate the end of Greg's sentence.

The tone softens, as if every effort were being made to keep the literal question about to be asked from sounding the least bit condescending. "Greg, you say you owed your patient a cure. But why?"

"Because my patient trusted me with her life," Greg snaps. "I accepted responsibility when I scheduled her first biopsy. I took responsibility for each treatment that followed. Why not take responsibility in the end? Of course, I couldn't tell her I failed her (the hospital lawyers would freak out!), but I sure wanted to."

"Idealism is admirable. Hope—the physician's *and* the patient's—is nurtured by a fervent sense of purpose."

Greg nods, his confidence returning. "I won't be satisfied with anything short of victory."

"That's good. When a sense of failure energizes your mind and soul, it inoculates you against burnout. But be careful: a death-is-failure attitude can lead many unsuspecting physicians to a draining disappointment that drags them into apathy or despair."

"What about my patient's disappointment?" Greg asks, wrapping the fingers of his left hand around his glass of water. "She was so disappointed and sad at the end."

"Ah. Your patient. How do you think she would have responded if you'd told her you failed her?"

Greg slowly twirls his straw between his right thumb and index finger, as if rewinding memories in search of his patient's answer.

"Patients at the end of their lives often ride an emotional seesaw of hopeful acceptance, struggling to make peace with impending death while still holding on to hope for recovery. Or, at least, trying to hold on to their dignity."

Greg asks, "Wouldn't my taking responsibility for the outcome free my patient of any possible shred of self-blame?"

"Maybe for some patients. For others, a physician's declaration of failure might arouse doubt. They might begin asking themselves if perhaps a different doctor or treatment would have succeeded (and saved them). This notion at any level of consciousness can feed patients' self-recriminations about their choices."

"Or, I suppose, a sense of being cheated out of time they might have—could have, should have—had." Greg adds.

"The danger is that physicians' failures often become their patients' failures. When your treatments lead to cure, your patients claim, 'I beat cancer!' When your best treatments don't work, your patients might conclude, 'I failed my doctor. I failed to get well and win the battle.' Your noble attempt to relieve your patient's feelings of failure may, in fact…"

"…worsen them," Greg concludes, his shoulders slumping. "So then, when I have nothing to offer but hope and caring, what do I say?"

"These conversations can't be scripted."

After a long silence, Greg proposes, "Maybe I could have said that my patient and I did everything possible to give her the best chance. How I wish things were different and wish we had more. How some things—unfortunately, but unavoidably—are beyond anyone's control." Greg pauses to take a sip of water before continuing, "I could admire my patient for doing the best she could, pointing out that nobody can do better than best."

"And then?"

"I'll stop talking. And listen. I'll listen with an ear toward understanding what my patient needs right now. Should she mention one of the small victories we shared along the way—and I hope she does—I'll honor it. Before leaving her room, I will reassure her of the one thing I can guarantee: 'Whatever happens, I will continue to care for you *and* about you.'"

The waiter interrupts, "Excuse me, sir. Are you okay? Are you ready to order, or are you waiting for someone?"

"I'm fine. Good, actually. And, no, it's just me today." Putting on his glasses and picking up his menu, Greg smiles warmly at the waiter, "Half a minute more, and I'll be ready."

***

Cure sometimes. Relieve often. Comfort always. In medicine, "sometimes" occurs far more often today than when Osler wrote his dictum. But to the patient's last breath and the end of time, "always" remains absolute. Patients can receive the best of science and caring, and die. The only failure may be that of gifted healers not recognizing triumph and sharing it with their patients.

- When we've done all we can, our avoiding any suggestion we failed avoids burdening patients who might then doubt their choices.
- We help patients heal by reassuring them, "The best all of us can do is the best we can do."
- We help patients find meaning by allowing them to share memories of triumph and validating their meaningful relationships with members of the healthcare team.

Misguided Metaphor

Patients often talk of "arming themselves" to "fight" or "defeat" their diseases. While battle imagery works well for many people, it can create unintended problems.

How can they say that? Of all people, they should know better. I excuse elderly people, realizing they remember when cancer was "the Big C" and patients didn't have much chance. I forgive young adults, too, assuming their naiveté about terminal illness. But when a respected national organization—especially a survivorship group—announces that So-and-so "lost her battle" with cancer, I explode.

The battle metaphor doesn't work well for me as a patient, but that's not the upsetting part. It's this notion of losing. To lose means to give up or otherwise fail to win a match of wits, brawn or nerve. Whether on a sports field, in an artillery zone or at a tribal meeting of television's *Survivor*, to lose your battle means you've been defeated. Someone else won, and you lost.

In some battles, the outcome depends purely on the combatants' talents, decisions and efforts. In other battles, luck plays a crucial role. What about illness?

My doctors beat my original lymphoma into remission with "big guns" chemotherapy and bombarded my first recurrence with radiation. Through it all, I armed myself with good nutrition, exercise, prayer, a support group and a positive attitude.

Soon after being diagnosed with my second recurrence, I screamed to the sky, "What am I doing wrong?" Hearing such an absurd question escape from my own mouth shocked me into realizing the only thing wrong was how I was thinking about my disease.

As a physician, I had intimate knowledge of illness as intrinsic to the human condition, along with pain, loss and awareness of our mortality. I knew that my battle—if we must call it that—between me and my malignant cells would likely determine the number of my days. But the important battle ahead was that which would define me as a person: namely, the fight to find fortitude, courage, wisdom and patience in hard times. The human struggle after cancer lies in creating meaning and joy in whatever time we have.

Metaphors serve a useful function, clarifying ideas and motivating people with graphic visuals. The declaration of a "War on Cancer" in 1971 helped funnel government funds toward needed research. And every day, personalized "battle plans" have encouraged many newly diagnosed patients to get second opinions, consider clinical trials as treatment options, eat healthful diets and ask for emotional support. Clearly, battle imagery can nourish hope and prompt effective action.

So why do I get worked up about "lost her battle"? Because in the context of end-stage illness, this metaphor is seriously flawed in two ways. First, no matter what disease or injury engaged the patient in a battle to the end, no victor emerges from the battlefield of hospice. In the case of cancer, for example, disordered sheets of cells with bizarre nuclei don't stand on podiums with gold medals around their surface antigens. Rather, malignancies—now powerless—are buried with the patient. Second and far more important is the harm this metaphor does to patients in their final days and to their loved ones left behind. Dying does not mean a patient has lost.

The first century Roman writer Marcus Seneca said, "Fire is the test of gold, adversity of strong men." Before my cancer diagnosis, I saw myself as a doctor, wife, mother of three, mediocre violinist and terrible humorist. Yet it was only after cancer, when I was sick and bald, or closing my medical practice, or gearing up for yet another round of treatment, that I discovered essential truths about myself.

To say that a patient who died has lost the battle is to insult the memories of people who inspire me today. Ellen, Lloyd and Nancy are only three of my many friends and acquaintances who nobly faced illness and death, each with a unique blend of hope and acceptance, humor, humility, fire and grace. Cancer failed to rob any of them of their dignity and humanity.

When you hear that someone died of multiple sclerosis, diabetes or some other disease, all you know is that he or she died. The person who dies of incurable disease or some complication of treatment, but who obtained good medical care and connected lovingly with friends and family to the end, has triumphed. The person who is cured, but who lives with bitterness about aftereffects or in constant fear of recurrence, has succumbed.

For me, triumph over illness is measured by how you live, not how long. Put another way, what matters is what you live for, not what you die of.

> - We comfort patients by reminding them that we can only affect, not control, the outcome.
> - We dignify patients by applauding their efforts to get well and live as fully as possible.
> - We help patients find meaning by reflecting that triumph is measured by how one lives.

On Purpose

Purpose is the stuff of philosophers and theologians. Yet when evaluating patients, clinicians' inquiry about patients' sense of purpose may yield important clues. Spiraling anxiety, depression or fatigue may be related to patients' struggles with competing purposes, loss of purpose, or purpose-driven actions that are not wise or healthy.

During the disorienting weeks after a diagnosis of serious illness, patients often ask "Why me?" This question never once enters my mind in the weeks after my diagnosis, which I attribute to all I've seen over the years as a physician. If anything, "Why not me?" Then, after weeks of wrestling with fear of death, an unexpected concern erupts: "What if I survive?"

Suddenly I am grappling with existential questions of purpose. I reach for the idea that this journey through illness will offer me useful insights about my patients. Assigning purpose to my ordeal beyond physical healing lessens the aloneness of lying in a scanner and the sucking pain of bone marrow aspirations. But finding purpose in my *illness* only increases my need to figure out the purpose in my *life*.

My answers begin when much-needed sleep is disrupted by my anxiety-induced and medication-tampered dreams. The varied details always fade within seconds of my awakening, but their collective message is unshakable: "Wendy, the purpose of life is to help others."

Some friends insist this insight comes directly from God. Others believe it is simply the soul-less expression of the complex neurochemical workings of my drugged and stressed brain. Whatever, the notions of goodness and of helping others give me direction. But the infinite number of possibilities nearly paralyzes me. I wonder *how* I should be helping others. I feel unsure of what I should be doing right this minute.

I've always prided myself on living purposefully. Goal-oriented and driven, I've appreciated the power of purpose to clear a straight path through all the confusing and tempting choices and to confer a sense of control. Now stripped of my white coat and freed of my frenzied schedule, I feel lost.

Not a week goes by that some kindhearted person doesn't assure me, "Wendy, I know you are going to survive because you have a purpose on earth." Nodding politely, I resent the unintended implication that my friends who died didn't have a purpose. However, the corollary catches my attention: I can pursue purpose *because* I am surviving.

Of all my possible purposes on earth, my children are clearly my top priority. As I undergo tests and treatments, knowing I must do all I can to be here for them releases fountains of courage and fortitude I never knew I had.

Physically unable to care for my patients, I discover I can write guides for them. The wordsmithing distracts me from my nausea and pain. My favorite joke—"I can't die because I'm in the middle of a book project."—helps me feel in control. The more I repeat it the greater confidence I enjoy. Most importantly, finding new purpose as a writer preserves my sense of self as a physician, keeping me grounded when everything else feels in flux.

I am riding the wave of purpose when a telephone call from a mentor-friend alerts me to potential problems with purpose. He's been living with metastatic disease for over a year. I admire his passion for helping survivors, and I want to emulate his example of living joyfully no matter what is happening medically.

Partway through our conversation, I press the receiver against my ear, his words nearly drowned out by the whining of his son in the background, "Da Da! Me need you." The episode sensitizes me to the cries of my own children and the danger of competing purposes.

On more than one occasion, I've stayed up too late supporting other survivors or writing at my computer instead of shutting down and getting enough rest. Seeing how I'm swayed to ignore my children or my body, the intoxicating power of purpose begins to scare me.

I almost can't believe it when other survivors, swept up in the emotional high of gratitude and purpose, quit their jobs, spend money they don't have, alienate loved ones or make life-altering decisions without thinking through the potential negative consequences.

The culture of the illness warrior feeds dangerous illusions of purpose. The extraordinary accomplishments of high-profile patients can make any effort short of running a marathon or founding a national non-profit feel insignificant. And though I am always kidding when I make the crack about my book projects protecting me from dying, other patients seem genuinely convinced that their devotion to purpose confers invincibility. Worrisome symptoms are ignored. Follow-ups are neglected.

To help me find balance between competing purposes, I seek counseling with a social worker and with my rabbi. I come to see that on some days my primary purpose might be just to get through treatment. Fulfilling my purpose, at times, might demand I decline invitations to interesting survivorship projects to make room for embracing my non-cancer life. Above all else, I must guard against a sense of purpose backfiring and hindering my recovery.

I can't imagine living without purpose. It would be like hugging air. Illness has taught me that self-care is the first step toward fulfilling my purpose. Then whatever I am doing, if my words are said on purpose and my actions are done on purpose, I am living fully.

- To address a patient's purpose is to acknowl-edge the person as well as the disease.
- Briefly exploring the idea of purpose may help in the evaluation of patients who are struggling emotionally or appear inexplica-bly worn down.
- Referrals to social workers, clergy or other counselors may help patients in matters of the soul.

Mother, May I?

While clinicians are giving orders and writing prescriptions, patients are often struggling with a sense of loss of control over their body and their world. Every day, clinicians' words and actions exacerbate or alleviate this distress.

"You may take five giant steps," my big sister yelled.

"Mother, may I?" I called from the other end of our backyard.

"No! But you may go back two baby steps."

This children's game was one of my favorites, until I realized the outcome had nothing to do with skill or luck. Disturbed by activities that nurtured tyrannical tendencies, I stopped playing and all but forgot about mother-may-I until 30 years later.

A few months into my first course of chemotherapy, one of my girlfriends was helping me at home while my husband was teaching his Tuesday evening class. I re-member watching Vicki, standing with her back to the upright piano and ordering my three little ones on the other side of the room.

"Becky, you may take five giant steps," Vicki said.

A voice in my head mimicked her inflection, "Wendy, you may take five giant steps and start seeing your patients again."

"Mother, may I?" my daughter asked.

My imaginary "me" asked, "Doctor, may I?"

"No! But you may go back two baby steps."

"No, but you may go back to the chemoclinic."

It is no fun when illness shatters illusions of control. For me, a solo practitioner, the crash was humbling. Over the years, my delusion of control had grown stronger each time nurses followed my orders, pharmacists filled my prescriptions, and patients' illnesses yielded to my therapies. Until my diagnosis—and I'm embarrassed to admit this—a little part of me actually believed I'd willed my labors and deliveries to occur on my days off, as I'd promised my patients throughout my pregnancies.

My distress over losing control wasn't an aberration. Many people who are newly diagnosed with cancer suffer from a mildly unsettling to an utterly disabling sense of loss of control over their body and their world. At the very least, patients have to be *where* you tell them *when* you tell them, and then they have to do *what* you tell them *the way* you tell them.

Just for a moment, imagine lying still in a scanner's coffin-like donut hole on an unyielding flat surface— euphemistically called a scanner "couch"—and being commanded to "Take a breath. H—o—l—d it…breathe. Take a breath. H—o—l—d it…."

In situations where cooperation and compliance improve the chance of recovery, giving up control helps patients regain control. As a patient, I understood that, intellectually. I believed it, too.

But the emotional cost was great. Even the littlest, silliest loss of control could be upsetting, such as the time I was carrying a lawn chair to one of my kids' sports games. One parent said, "Wendy, let me carry that for you," and another just started grabbing the chair from my hands, commanding, "You shouldn't be carrying that!"

The unintended consequence of their noble actions was to strip me of my autonomy at a time when I was already feeling innumerable losses and was trying to hold on to one side of me that was not "a patient." Instead of feeling comforted and relieved, I felt more anxious. "Do I look too sick to carry a lawn chair? Am I too sick?"

An essential element of quality care is restoring and maintaining patients' sense of control. Years ago, a survivor in my support group told a true story of an angel who knew how to do this. The man's story begins when his oncologist—a colleague of mine named Gabriel—starts to leave his hospital room at the end of a visit. "Hey, Doc, would you mind leaving the door open a little?" he asks.

Obliging, Gabriel adjusts the door, leaving it open a few inches before he walks away. As the storyteller described it to me, "Ten seconds later, my doctor returns, peeks his head into my room and asks, 'Is this okay?' He then playfully opens the door an additional three inches. 'Maybe this is better?' and then closes the door an inch, teasing, 'Better now?'"

The patient was not only amused, which was the oncologist's primary aim, but also comforted and strengthened by the many messages of this simple act: "I care about you to the inch. You are in charge of this. You are worth my time and effort."

Early in my survivorship, I realized that whether we were talking about how I used my time or what I ate or when I went to sleep, I needed others to let me hold on to control of things that were well within my grasp and to ask my permission before helping out or taking over.

This notion is particularly important when patients are dying and their world is gradually and inexorably contracting. I'm reminded of an ancient Jewish prayer: Please don't let me die before I die.

From the moment of diagnosis on, healthcare professionals help patients take a giant step toward healing by preserving their autonomy whenever possible and reasonable. Many times, all it takes is a simple "May I?"

- We dignify patients by making requests instead of demands whenever possible.
- We honor patients by asking permission before proceeding.

Conversation 2008

Will, Jessie, and Becky were one, three and five years old when I was first diagnosed with cancer in 1990. Although none of my physicians were pediatricians, they played a vital role in helping my children through my illness, as illustrated by this interview.

Becky: "So, you want to know what it was like for us? I was a kindergartner when my mom got cancer. To be honest, much of the first few years of her illness are a blur. I just remember feeling really scared and hating everything having to do with cancer, doctors and hospitals."

Jessie: "I was only three years old, so I wasn't scared like Becky. I didn't know to be."

Will: "Since I was a baby when it all started, for me Mom has always had cancer. All I know is that the sicker Mom got, the grumpier Dad got, and I felt helpless to do anything to make it better. Like Jessie, I didn't feel scared. Well, not until I was in 11th grade and her cancer came back again. My sisters were off at college, calling me at all hours for updates and reassurance. While dealing with high-school drama and stressing out about college, I was also worrying about my mom."

Becky: "What helped me most? That's simple: My parents always told me the truth. Sure, I still worried about her...her dying. But I never worried about what might be going on that they weren't telling us (or that they were lying). For instance, Mom and I were shopping one day and saw a lady wearing a scarf. We both could tell she was bald. I said, 'Mom, you are never gonna need scarves again, right?' My mom answered, 'I hope not, but if I do, I'll wear pretty scarves like that lady.' Part of me was furious that she refused to say what I wanted to hear: 'We're done with cancer.' But I was glad she was truthful."

Jessie: "Me, too. I'd always rather know the truth."

Will: "The truth helped us in good times, too. Once I overheard her on the phone say something about scans. After she hung up, I asked, 'Everything all right?' She said, 'Yes, I'm fine. A neighbor's dad has cancer.' That was all I needed; I didn't worry another second."

Becky: "Not another second, Will? I don't think so."

Will: "No, I meant I didn't worry anymore about that phone call."

Becky: "It also helped that each time her cancer came back, my mom and dad made a big deal about how she was getting 'the best' possible treatments. That she had 'the best' possible chance."

Jessie: "And how they had lots of hope."

Will: "They also told us how they'd help us. I can still hear them saying, 'We got through it before. We can get through it again.'"

Jessie: "Our mom did things to make cancer fun, too."

Becky: "Oh, please. Cancer is never fun. Name one fun thing."

Jessie: "Our chemo-days box."

Becky: "Oh yeah! I forgot about that: the shoebox filled with activity books and *Polly Pocket* toys. We could open it only on her chemo days."

Will: "And do you remember how Mom brought home the plastic mask they used at the hospital when she had radiation therapy? We played 'radiation,' using the TV remote as the control switch to zap each other."

Jessie: "Don't forget 'Mommy-and-me' days. We each got a day with mom all by ourselves. I think she did it because she felt guilty."

Becky: "Listen, no matter what they did to try to make it fun or make up for it, home basically sucked when Mom had recurrences and needed treatment. I feel bad about it now, but I spent as much time as I could at my friends' houses. And looking back, I know I said and did stupid things that just added to the stress at home."

Will: "You know what, Becky? They yelled at us sometimes even when we didn't deserve it."

Becky: "Yeah, sometimes. Actually, we didn't deserve any of it: the bald and tired mom, the cancelled birthday parties and summer vacations, the separations when mom was treated in California. Now, of course, I know it wasn't anybody's fault."

Jessie: "Mom and Dad told us over and over again that it wasn't our fault."

Becky: "I guess when I was little I knew it in my head but didn't believe it in my heart. If you had given me a quiz, I'd have gotten the right answer: 'It is not my fault Mom got sick (or had to go to the hospital again, or whatever).' But for years, I still kept thinking, 'It has to be *somebody's* fault.' On the bad days, I did worry that, maybe, it was because of something I was doing wrong."

Jessie: "One thing that helped me was hearing how great Mom's doctors and nurses were."

Becky: "Me too. That was something I could believe, especially after we went to see Mom get radiation.

The nurses at the hospital treated us special, lifting each of us up to see our mom through the little glass window. You know, if I could tell doctors and nurses only one thing, it would be, 'Do your best. That is our mom or dad sitting on your exam table."

Will: "I think you should tell your patients about the cool groups, books and Web sites for kids whose mom or dad has cancer. Because by helping our parents, you help us kids."

Jessie: "Here's my two cents: Please ask about us."

Becky: "And don't just ask, 'How are your kids?' 'Cause they'll say 'Fine.' You need to ask, 'How are you helping your kids?' That sends the message that cancer is hard on the kids, too."

Jessie: "I second that."

Will: "I third it."

- We help patients hold on to their identities as parents by asking how they are helping their children deal with the family illness.
- We help patients feel confident about helping their children by guiding them to useful resources.
- We give meaning to a family's struggles by explaining, "The greatest gift we can give our children is not protection from the world, but the confidence and tools to cope and grow with all that life has to offer."

Final Good-byes

Saying good-bye to patients whose care is being transferred to hospice presents a number of challenges to clinicians.

Dr. Solor lifts the cold, full coffee pot at the deserted nurses' station, thinking, *"This is odd."* Just then a muffled swell of laughter rises from the conference room at the end of the hall, and he remembers.

A familiar husky voice from behind startles him. "The quiet feels eerie, eh?"

With a bright smile, Dr. Solor turns to her and offers his filled cup, "Coffee, Dr. Katz? It's cold; you'll have to nuke it."

"No thanks. I'm headed over to Theresa's retirement luncheon. Want to join me?"

"You go ahead. Dictations are calling," he says, tipping his head toward a computer screen.

"Aw, c'mon. The dictations can wait; today is Theresa's last day."

"Maybe in a bit…"

"Alright," she says, but she doesn't make a move.

"I'll miss Theresa," he offers, as if asked to explain. "Truth be told, I just never know quite what to say at those things."

Dr. Katz nods and repeats, "Alright."

Dr. Solor could tell from the tone of her voice and the look on her face that she is thinking about more than Theresa's retirement.

"Speaking of good-byes," Dr. Katz says tentatively, "I spoke with our patient, Jeff, yesterday."

"You did? Is there a problem with hospice?"

"No, no. He's very happy with hospice."

"Good," Dr. Solor is pleased. "That's good to hear."

"In fact," Dr. Katz says, "Jeff mentioned how grateful he is to have them."

"Then why did Jeff call you?"

"He didn't. I called him."

Dr. Solor leans against the chair by the computer, feeling uneasy and unsure why.

Dr. Katz continues, "Medically, things are going smoothly." Dr. Katz clears her throat. "You need to know: Jeff is pretty upset with you."

Dr. Solor's stomach drops. He has no clue what she's talking about.

"It seems you never said good-bye."

"What!?" Dr. Solor blanches and his mouth drops open.

"I was shocked, too," says Dr. Katz. "You guys had such a great relationship."

"Good-bye?" Dr. Solor looks confused.

Nodding, Dr. Katz says, "Apparently at his last office visit, he asked about his next appointment, and you said something to the effect of 'You don't need another appointment. Hospice will take care of everything from now on.'"

"Okay." Dr. Solor is visibly distressed. "And?"

His mind scrambles to understand. *"I remember exactly where I was standing when I explained that hospice has the specialized skills needed for him to get the best possible care."*

Dr. Solor shakes his head. "I guess I'm missing something."

"All I know is Jeff feels abandoned," Dr. Katz responds. "He talked about how all these years he thought you cared. How you helped him through difficult decisions, treatments and crises."

A lopsided smile crosses Dr. Solor's lips. On the bulletin board in his office, somewhere among the collage of pictures sent by other patients, is an image of Jeff. He's proudly holding up his "this big" fish, the feisty trout Jeff caught shortly after his prolonged hospitalization—half of which he spent intubated in ICU.

Dr. Katz concludes, "It's just not a good situation. Jeff feels hurt. Now he thinks he was mistaken all these years—that you must not really care."

"How could he possibly think I don't care?" Dr. Solor is stunned. "I do care."

"Of course, and I told Jeff how much you care about him."

"Did you explain why I didn't say good-bye?"

Dr. Katz leans toward Dr. Solor. "I just repeated what I knew: I assured Jeff that you do care about him."

Dr. Solor drops his gaze to the floor, mumbling, "I thought what I did was right, but I guess…" He retreats into his own world, straining to recall every nuance of every word exchanged at Jeff's final visit.

Dr. Katz reaches gently for his elbow, "C'mon, Doc. Let's go to that luncheon."

***

This story is not purely hypothetical. A friend of mine had glowing esteem and gratitude for his oncologist's care throughout his years and rounds of treatment. This friend was devastated by his final visit with his oncologist.

I reminded my friend that many people—not just physicians—have trouble saying good-bye. But I could not account for the abrupt ending that left him feeling abandoned. My efforts to comfort my friend felt hollow.

Under any circumstances, saying good-bye is emotional if the relationship is meaningful, especially if the parting may be forever. Yet I cannot think of a single non-medical situation where departures are not marked with words or rituals of closure.

For physicians, final good-byes can be uncomfortable. They dramatize the limits of physicians' abilities to cure. Some physicians equate saying "good-bye" with admitting defeat. Others, fearing their patients might interpret these potent words as two nails in the coffin, deliberately avoid "good-bye" so as not to risk extinguishing patients' hope.

To leave room for patients' hope, physicians can say something like, "I'll be keeping my eyes open for you. If a new treatment becomes available (or if your condition unexpectedly improves), you can leave hospice and I'll resume your care."

As for softening the good-bye, you can let them know, "I'll be checking in on you through the hospice nurses." Better yet, tell them you will call them in a week or two, socially and just to say "Hi." If your schedule doesn't easily allow post-discharge communications, maybe you can find some way to say, "With hospice taking care of your needs now, I won't be caring for you anymore. But I'll still be caring about you."

The transition to hospice is emotionally complex. Whether a patient is adjusting well or not, physician-patient communications can too easily become confused. A final good-bye can be healing for patients. And for physicians, too. Because the pain of good-bye acknowledges all that is good.

- Patients know they matter if we make time to say good-bye.
- Patients feel valued if we express our emotions with words or tears.
- We help patients heal by caring *about* them when we are no longer caring *for* them.

CHAPTER 5

Happiness

"…we are here not to get all we can out of life for ourselves, but to try to make the lives of others happier."

Sir William Osler

"This is it," I remember thinking after weaning my third child. "The training, planning, building, hoping and waiting are finally over."

My medical practice was thriving and my family was complete. As clichéd as it sounds, I was flying high with the sense that I could begin living my dream. And I was determined to live it joyfully.

"Happily ever after" for me meant caring for patients and raising my family. As I saw it, the only obstacle to happiness now was finding a healthy balance between the two consuming worlds I loved so much. Unfortunately, I had taken only the first steps to achieve that balance when I developed cancer.

Throughout that first year as a patient, I learned a great deal about obtaining knowledge, nourishing hope, taking effective action and finding meaning. But it wasn't until the following year, when my cancer recurred and I had to close my medical practice permanently, that I stopped to think about happiness in any meaningful way. From what felt like the ruins of the life I'd so painstakingly built, I asked myself, "How can I find happiness now?"

Luckily for me, it was always a question of "how," not "if." Many of my patients had taught me by example that happiness is possible when life is not what you hoped for or prepared for or expected or wanted. What I hadn't fully appreciated was how much work it takes to pursue happiness in the setting of illness.

So what is happiness, anyway? One useful definition is "a state of well-being characterized by pleasant emotions ranging from contentment and tranquility to extreme joy and ecstasy." I like this definition because it emphasizes that a patient's happiness can be as unique as his or her fingerprints. And while "feeling happy" usually refers to emotions experienced at one moment in time, I see "being happy" as an overarching sense of wholeness that makes you glad to be alive.

Clearly happiness cuts to the core of our work as clinicians. After all, what's the point of healing patients' bodies if they aren't glad to be alive? With modern medicine making survival after devastating illness or injury an everyday occurrence, ethical concerns about patients' quality of life and happiness have become everyday matters, too.

Most physicians' training focuses almost completely on patients' pathophysiology and psychopathology. But I was a graduate of the University of Rochester School of Medicine and Dentistry, a school that was decades ahead of its time in teaching and using the biopsychosocial model. From my first day of class, I was conditioned to see each patient as a whole person in the context of his or her life.

After I got sick, I took the biopsychosocial model one step further by concluding that addressing patients' happiness is an essential element of compassionate care. In addition, such care may benefit healthcare professionals too and reduce their own risk of professional burnout. This chapter illustrates how.

I open by painting a picture of a hospital room in which a patient is hosting a celebration. Many busy clinicians avoid such parties, especially if the patient is still at serious risk of complications or untimely death. "Time to Celebrate" shares a lesson I learned as a patient about finding happiness in the face of uncertainty.

The next two stories poke fun at patients' superstitions and false alarms. "Opal" invites busy clinicians to play with the idea that harmless superstitions, although unscientific, may be healing. "Duds" explores false alarms from a patient's point of view. The normal test results that bring clinicians relief can cause patients to feel distressed, which is why clinicians who address patients' reactions to false alarms may open opportunities for patients' celebrations.

My tone turns serious with "Saving My Self." In modern medical facilities, the twin pressures of time and technology are threatening to reduce patient care to faceless assembly-line work. Acknowledging patients' individuality and their lives outside their medical conditions becomes critical. This story underscores clinicians' role in preserving patients' sense of self, which is linked not only to patients' happiness but also to clinicians' sense of fulfillment, too.

Even a task as mundane as managing the office appointment book provides a way to preserve patients' sense of self. In "On Schedule," you'll see why what appears to be a problem of logistics—when to schedule tests, procedures and follow-up visits—can, in fact, be a problem of joy.

From the time we are little, we mark especially joyful times by exchanging gifts. Although only a tiny facet of clinician-patient relationships, patients giving gifts to doctors has been under increasing scrutiny. You'll read how my opinion of patients giving gifts changed after I closed my medical practice.

Ironically, the final story of this book is the first creative non-fiction I ever wrote. I had just returned from visiting one of my call partners, who was a patient in the hospital. I knew when I had said good-bye and had thrown him a kiss from the foot of the bed that it would be the last time I'd see him. My mentor and friend was a gifted and compassionate physician. It felt too soon. And so wrong. I had to find some way to make sense of it, so I wrote "Patent Pending: The Measure of a Life." After my friend died, this fable took on a life of its own, comforting mourners with the memories of lives well-lived.

Every day, in the rush of ordering tests and prescribing treatments, clinicians brush up against death. As I explain in my poem, "The View from Remission," it is precisely because tomorrow is uncertain that celebrating today makes all the sense in the world. No matter how busy we are, we have to make time for happiness. By helping patients in their pursuit of happiness, we further our mission of healing.

Time to Celebrate

Knowing all the potential problems of recovery, we don't relax until our patients are completely out of danger. But the desire for greater certainty before celebrating can shut down opportunities for joy.

Charlie manages his escape and walks away briskly. I follow close behind. As soon as the mirrored elevator door closes, Charlie shakes off the sting of high-fives and exuberant handshakes before rubbing his temple with his index and middle fingers. The rockin' party has clearly left him agitated.

"What's wrong?" I ask, wondering if he was bothered by the over-crowded room where the guests are still laughing and talking too loudly, or by their noise spilling out into the hallway and disturbing other patients.

"I hate those parties," he says, tilting his head in the direction of our last patient.

A bright and caring physician, Charlie cringes when he mentions the sea of sparkling-apple-juice-filled plastic cups hoisted in his honor. Now I know why his voice sounded spirited and his smile was broad, but no crinkles appeared around the corners of his eyes when he lifted his ersatz-bubbly and toasted, "Cheers!"

Alone with me and our reflections, Charlie's candor is definitive. "It is not time to celebrate. They're in denial. *If* Dave makes it through the next four to six months, then maybe…."

A beeping from Charlie's belt interrupts. He looks down. The door opens, and he's gone.

Not time? Sure, Dave's not out of the woods. I know that. His disease and the experimental procedure used to treat it put him at risk of a host of life-threatening post-discharge problems, not the least of which is, of course, that his disease doesn't respond and kills him. Only some of the patients who go home will survive long term. But is it wrong to celebrate now?

Celebrations are not just fun festivities; they serve a purpose: to mark special occasions. (Whatever the celebrant considers "special," that is. Heck, as a kid I celebrated my half-birthdays.) We celebrate whatever, whenever. I remember years when I was the designated Turkey-day doctor, so my family made Thanksgiving on Wednesday. No problem. The link between an occasion and its party is in our minds and hearts.

In contrast to birthdays and holidays, which come and go according to the date, celebrations of achievements are conditional. To put medical school behind me wasn't enough to warrant a graduation party; I also had to pass my exams and earn my diploma. Years later, unlike my pregnant friends (and in accordance with my heritage), I set a date for my baby shower only after I was rocking my healthy newborn in my arms. In other words, I'd pause to party only after the challenge was over, the outcome determined, and I'd gotten what I wanted or ended up where I'd hoped to be.

Implicit in these achievements—these endings to challenging and uncertain times—were joyful new beginnings. My spanking new medical degree and my infant daughter were tangible proof of the promise of a long and prosperous future.

What about Dave's future, though? Statistically speaking, his hospital discharge is hardly a paid and punched ticket to tomorrow. If the goal is remission, maybe, as Charlie suggested, Dave should wait a few months to see if the treatment works—until he's sure it is time to celebrate.

The elevator door opens again, and I smell piping hot sourdough bread. Walking through the hospital cafeteria line, I reminisce about a San Francisco dinner long ago. My lymphoma had recurred a second time, only two-and-a-half years after my original diagnosis. With my long-term prognosis not looking good, my future had all but disappeared. At least, it felt that way. On that warm evening, I was discharged from Stanford University Medical Center after receiving investigational therapy in a Phase I trial. Stepping outside the hospital, my husband I were blinded by the California sunshine.

I told Ted, "No! We are not going to just 'wait and see,'" (as my doctors had suggested), "but live and see." Impelled by an urge to celebrate, Ted and I went out to dinner where, clinking together our water glasses, we toasted.

"I made it to today." Unlike when I'd signed the consent form, we could relax about all the potential complications—including death—which hadn't happened during treatment. The medicine was now in my veins. Whatever the ultimate outcome, we had succeeded in doing what we could to stack the odds in my favor.

"I am going home today." By definition, hospital discharge meant my condition was getting better, not worse. And no matter how superb the nursing care, there's no place like home.

"I have today." My cancer didn't make life uncertain; it exposed the uncertainty of life. In losing my sense of tomorrow, I appreciated what time I had—in a way I never had before—and found today.

Celebrations infuse meaning and joy where calendars coldly mark the passing of time. A uniquely human endeavor, cake and balloons and music and laughter create a sensory feast intended to trigger or enhance the innate high of an anniversary or accomplishment.

When times are good, celebrations keep me grateful. And humble. When times are tough, not everything or every day is celebrated. But occasional celebrations acknowledge all that is right in the world and help me find happiness. And hope.

I put down my fork and ask myself, "Is Dave in denial?" Hardly. Maybe he's scared, wanting distraction. Or exhausted and hopeless, needing a boost. Or excited, pumped up by a premonition about remission. Whatever, it is precisely because tomorrow is uncertain that celebrating today makes all the sense in the world.

Almost done with my lunch, I look up and see Charlie entering the cafeteria. "Hey, Charlie!" I wave him over.

"I'm going to have a cup of coffee. Can you join me? I'd like to talk."

> - We help patients find happiness by encouraging them to celebrate in the face of uncertainty.
> - We honor patients by joining in their celebrations.
> - We recharge our batteries by appreciating the small victories.

Opal

Healthcare professionals provide the vital link to science-based therapies. That doesn't mean we have to condemn every little superstition.

I'm going only 30 m.p.h. when the light turns yellow, but it's too late. Already at the corner and committed, with a pickup truck close on my tail, I step on the gas. My teenage daughter riding shotgun scrunches up in a ball, her right hand holding the grip above her window, her left thumb and index finger pinching closed her nostrils, her eyes shut tight and her cheeks puffed out. As soon as we pass through the intersection, she resumes her usual sitting position and animated chatter.

"What was that?" I ask while gently braking for the next red light.

"What?"

"Back there. The sudden...you know...your whole—(I shut my eyes, clamp my nose and puff out my cheeks)—thing."

"Oh, that?" She grins. "Running a yellow light is good luck. I was making a wish."

I usually chuckle at her knocking on our butcher-block kitchen table to counter the bad karma should I mention some dreadful possibility, such as off-kilter numbering when bubbling-in her SAT answer sheet or— gasp—showing up in the same prom dress as Robyn.

Such scrunching and knocking are part of a bountiful repertoire of tics and rituals she draws on to manipulate the joystick of Lady Luck.

"Darling, you know this is total silliness."

"I know, Ma. It doesn't hurt anything."

"Maybe not," I respond.

But I'm not so sure. When it comes to illness, some patients attach significance to coincidence. It worries me when a patient's outlook—positive or negative—seems shaped more by the symbolic meaning of a doctor's name or the floor number of the clinic than by the statistics.

My daughter taps the face of my car's digital clock announcing 2:22 then closes her eyes and brings her consecrated fingers to her lips for a kiss. With twelve repeating-digit wish opportunities on the clock every day, why wait for birthday candles?

Since my cancer diagnosis when my children were young, I've strived to use my unwanted illness to teach them healthy life skills. I'm perhaps most proud of demonstrating an acceptance of and adjustment to uncertainty, such as that surrounding my repeated recurrences of lymphoma.

When it comes to making medical decisions, I desperately want my children to become adults who appreciate the value of science-based information. So I've consistently pooh-poohed superstitions—theirs and others'—and have offered a strong model: "Pure magical thinking, sweetie. *I* don't believe in such nonsense."

They've also seen how, as a physician-survivor, I've worked hard to distinguish good science from junk and to encourage other patients to do the same. My zeal stems from my concerns about anything that gets in the way of obtaining good care.

This stand against superstition is rocked by an epiphany while I'm casually reading about opals, the birthstone for October. I learn that for centuries, from Romans to Asians, the opalescent silica has been treasured as a healing stone and powerful symbol of hope. "Wow," the hairs on my forearms suddenly stand erect.

With my birthday—October 18—an identifying statistic that helps to define "me," an excitement pulsates through my veins. You see, Hebrew letters represent numbers, and the Hebrew spelling for 18 is hey (eight) and yud (ten). This two-letter combination also spells "chai," the Hebrew word for "living." Which means I was born on "the hope of living."

The newfound symbolism adds oomph to the realistic hope of my science-based treatments, like a sprinkling of salt on a simmering stew. A pleasurable new calm takes me totally by surprise. So am I superstitious now? Hardly. I still walk blithely under ladders and have no qualms if a black cat crosses my path. I remain a hard-core scientist, completely convinced that my "chai" birthday in no way affects the efficacy of my cancer treatments or confers an iota of advantage in the healing potential of my body. I just like that I was born on October 18, a day some people consider the "hope of living." Fascinating.

Old wives' tales and mystical beliefs weave through every culture in every day and age. Thinking back to my medical practice, I couldn't crack down on patients' superstitions any more than I could ban daydreaming. In the setting of uncertainty and hardship, daydreams and superstitions invariably poke their way through the goal-directed daily grind.

Reveries and silly beliefs can add whimsy or inspiration to challenging times. As a physician, I needed to know and address only the ideas or images—real or imagined—that were making it more difficult for my patients to get good care or move forward.

We could argue about what it means when I now touch the digital clock on my dashboard and then raise my hand to my mouth for a kiss. Honestly, I think it's that the absurdity of what I'm doing reminds me of my silly kids. I won't argue if you suggest it gives me a sense of control. Whatever, wishing on time makes me smile. But if the light turns yellow, whether I decide to slow down or drive through, my eyes stay on the road and my hands remain on the wheel.

> - Finding out about our patients' superstitions may alert us to worrisome beliefs.
> - We help patients through difficult times by letting slide their harmless superstitions that bring comfort or joy.

Duds

We rejoice when test results prove a patient's worrisome symptom to be a false alarm. Then, depending on what the symptom is, we either reassure the patient that all is well or continue our evaluations, looking elsewhere for explanations. But in the face of good news, patients can become troubled.

False alarms remind me of Jo, a slender executive who was not the type to cry "wolf." One morning Jo called my office about blood in her stool. My receptionist heard Jo's distress and told her to hustle right over. In a flash, my patient was straightening her gown and watching me turn away with a small sample of her concern on my gloved finger. Seconds later, I turned back to Jo, smiling.

"Jo, what did you eat for dinner last night?"

"Baked chicken, mashed potatoes, green beans," she answered.

"Any dessert?" I prodded.

Jo slumped forward and dropped her face into her cupped hands. "I can't believe this." She peeked over her fingertips at me as she said, "Jello."

"Cherry?" I proposed, quite pleased with my finely tuned diagnostic acumen.

Jo blushed and looked at the floor.

"Hey now, be happy. I'm thrilled you don't need a workup."

Jo looked back at me and quipped, "Ok, Doc, as long as you're sure it's not *malignant* Jello." At her follow-up visits Jo enjoyed the intimacy, and I enjoyed the levity, of our private joke.

Not long after I "cured" Jo with a guaiac, I performed a routine exam on a middle-aged man, Mark, and noted a nodule in his prostate. Calmly, I explained the worrisome possibilities and suggested the best way to proceed. Mark stoically went through a series of tests that led to a needle-guided biopsy.

On the afternoon his path report reached my office, I dialed Mark's number myself, relishing my role as bearer of good news. Oh how I loved false alarms.

"Hi, Mark. It's Dr. Harpham. Your lump is completely benign. No cancer."

Expecting to hear relief and thanks, the shushing sound of my own breathing in my earpiece was puzzling.

"Hello?" I tested.

A flat voice responded, "Thanks. Bye." *Click.*

"Very weird," I thought.

Later that same afternoon, my assistant came into my office while I was dictating. Miming ferocity, she pointed to the blinking light signaling line two. As soon as I picked up the receiver, my cancer-free patient lambasted me for forcing him to go through the stress and expense of the workup "all for nothing."

Unlike Jo's little scare, Mark's false alarm was no laughing matter. I felt like Sisyphus at Mark's next few appointments, straining to rebuild his trust. In the years since, while caring for other patients and then while dealing with my own medical problems, I've seen how "case closed" for doctors and nurses can be a newly opened can of worms for the patient.

Soon after starting my latest round of cancer treatment, I am rubbing my aching lower back, and a lump unexpectedly rolls under my fingers. An inquisition between me and myself ensues: "What's this?" (I think it's a lump.) "Is the lump real?" (Lemme see. I'll re-examine it. Yes.) "Is it new?" (I've never felt it before.) "Is it important?" (I don't know, but the lump is right where I hurt.) "Should I call the doctor?"

My mind goes blank for a moment. I rely on the most appropriate mantra for the moment—"*Do the right thing, no matter how ridiculous you feel doing it.*" I call to make an appointment, so I can guide my oncologist's hand to just above my coccyx where Y marks the spot.

The next day, I'm looking at a view box with a radiologist. Scrolling back and forth through the thin-slice MRI images, he informs me that my "lump" is an unremarkable muscle insertion. Feeling flush in my cheeks—facial, not gluteal—I fumble for a "malignant jello"-like jest. Alas, "scan-confirmed lumpy butt" has no panache.

Now I feel ashamed for having sounded the alarm. I can't believe I've wasted my doctor's time and attention. I feel awful about worrying my husband unnecessarily. Self-doubt creeps in—How could I not know my own body?—and I vow to be more circumspect before reporting any new aches or bumps. I don't want to be a patsy for another dud.

Duds. Scattered among the many landmines of illness—complications, disease flares, and late effects—are duds. Red flags are raised by insignificant bounces of blood test results, over-read x-rays, transient benign adenopathy, and a host of signs and symptoms that come and go without explanation.

I've seen and had my share of duds. Some duds were serious, requiring surgical intervention for resolution. Others were embarrassing. Well, think about it: How would you like people checking out *your* keister?

Like Rodney Dangerfield, duds get no respect. But duds are important, and we can help patients deal with duds in healing ways. Preparing patients for the possibility of a false alarm helps these patients move on when the news is not what is feared. Acknowledging that the workup may seem like much ado about nothing helps patients accept the necessary tests and procedures as the cost of staying healthy.

We can remind patients that even when a dud occurs and means nothing is wrong, it does not mean the workup was a waste of resources. In medicine, a "negative" result is not "no news," but helpful news.

In fact, duds are good news worth celebrating. So, pat your patients on the back for doing the right thing to check out the problem. Reinforce that the next time something new pops up, you expect your patient to do the right thing again. And while doing the right thing, everyone can hope it's another dud.

- We preserve patient's dignity and encourage proper action in the future by reassuring them they did the right thing to call or come in.
- We strengthen patients' gratitude by reminding them of our patients with the same symptoms who wish theirs was a false alarm, too.
- We encourage joy by celebrating the false alarms.

Saving My Self

When I was first diagnosed, I was more prepared than the average patient for the many physical discomforts that awaited me. What took me totally by surprise was the threat to my sense of self.

My white coat and stethoscope lay draped over my chair, as if I'd slipped out of my office for a moment. Meanwhile, in another office, a surgeon was about to utter two words that would change my world forever: "It's back."

Soon after beginning treatment for this first cancer recurrence, I sat in a circle on the floor of my bedroom with a few girlfriends and my 7-year-old daughter, Becky. Chatting and laughing, we might have been mistaken for playing a child's game if it weren't for the stacks of "Dear Patient" letters announcing the closing of my medical practice.

While stuffing envelopes, one friend started to tell a story. "Since Wendy is a doctor..." My daughter interrupted, "Mom *used* to be a doctor."

As often happens when a child exposes the elephant in the room, an awkward twitter spread through my little party, and my girlfriends quickly changed the topic. But I was left wondering, "If I'm not a doctor, who am I?"

Over the next few weeks, my patients' charts scattered to doctors throughout the metroplex like feathers in the wind. At home, I fielded phone calls and read greeting cards from well-wishers expressing pity or sadness about my having cancer.

My insistence on resuming my pre-cancer exercise routine and plowing through issues of *New England Journal of Medicine* were transparent attempts to hold on to the old "me." But no amount of willpower could lessen my leg pain or overcome my need for midday rests. My thoughts slipped away like wet bars of soap, making it difficult for me to navigate familiar roads and social conversations—let alone to pursue clinical medicine. I had to figure out, "Who am I now?"

Know thyself is a dictum that emphasizes a vital task that begins in infancy when you learn to separate yourself from others. Even the ancient Greeks realized the value of continuing this process throughout life.

Each individual's perceptions, attitudes, beliefs and behaviors evolve slowly in response to new experiences and to all the changes of growing older. But a key element of "self" is continuity over time. So here's the challenge: bringing together your sense of your past, present and future. Unifying who *you were*, who *you are*, and who *you will be* into one person—*thyself*.

As a physician-survivor, I'm intrigued by the social side of "self," especially a modern theory of recognition suggesting that one's sense of self depends on recognition by others. I know "I am Wendy" when you say, "You are Wendy."

This idea helps explain why I became anxious after entering the hospital elevator one day. A colleague quickly shifted his gaze to his shoes, pretending he didn't see me. Intellectually I knew the problem was not me, no more than if a faucet's motion sensor failed to respond to my hand movement. My colleague was simply caught by surprise and didn't know what to say. Nevertheless, the episode was unsettling for me.

Reflecting on those days when my life felt consumed by illness, I realize the vital role my healthcare team played in saving my "self." Instead of pumping data into a computer or charting notes, my doctors looked me in the eye (poetically dubbed "the window to the soul") whenever they were listening or talking to me.

The oncology social worker helped me grieve my losses, so I could see and embrace all that remained. And she encouraged me to participate in a support group, knowing that veteran survivors would both serve as role models and give me the encouragement I needed to move forward.

The nurses who cared for me always asked about my family or my non-cancer-related activities while monitoring my vital signs and administering medications.

Whether it is part of their training or a natural instinct, oncology nurses are good at helping patients know who they are beyond their diseases.

Cancer can threaten more than patients' lives. One reason is that, unlike the gradual effects of aging, illness-related losses can occur almost overnight. Sexual dysfunction can destroy patients' sense of self as sexual partners. Physical changes that impair people's ability to fulfill usual roles threaten their sense of self as independent and responsible adults. Difficulties with mobility or communication can stifle their sense of self as social beings.

A healthy sense of self is essential to recovery after illness. So if a patient shows signs of anxiety or depression, or if a patient seems uninterested in recovery, consider the possibility of an underlying loss of *self,* and respond in *self*-healing ways.

When we treat patients with kindness, we help them regain *self*-respect and *self*-esteem. When we express belief in their abilities or refer them to educational and supportive resources, we help patients rebuild *self*-confidence. When our words and actions say, "You are you, no matter what is happening medically," we help patients let go of their "old normal" and recreate themselves in a "new normal" that integrates the changes and challenges accompanying their illness. In essence, addressing each patient as a unique individual dignifies the person with the disease.

Last week, someone asked my now 22-year-old daughter what I do. I was curious what she'd say. She answered, "She's a survivor. She used to be a doctor, but now she writes books for patients."

I suppose that's why I keep my white coat and stethoscope hanging just inside my closet door. They remind me of the doctor I used to be and the person I am today.

- We help patients heal by looking them in the eyes when talking with them.
- We help patients pursue happiness by helping them let go of their "old normal" and create a "new normal" that is the best it can be.
- We bring joy into our relationships with patients by inquiring about their lives outside their health.

On Schedule

Healthy Survivors live as fully as possible within the constraints of their illness. Patients look to us for expert guidance about how to evaluate their symptoms and treat their diseases. They also look to us for expert guidance about when to proceed.

"After you get dressed, you can go to the appointment desk to schedule the biopsy. And Julie, don't forget to leave a number where I can call you as soon as the results are in."

Her surgeon stands up and slowly backpedals toward the door. He's just spent 30 minutes ignoring his beeper, explaining every option regarding the evaluation of her suspicious lump.

"Anything else?" he asks as his left hand reaches behind him for the knob.

Julie shakes her head. The door creaks.

"Yeah, one last thing," she says, and her physician turns to face her squarely.

"If the biopsy *is* positive, how soon will I need to start treatment?"

"I don't want to speak for your oncologist, but *if* the biopsy is positive, he'll likely want to begin treatment right away." He reaches over and gives her hand a quick but caring squeeze before his nurse whisks him into the next exam room. Through the thin walls Julie can hear cheerful greetings, like those of old friends.

Julie slides off the exam table to change back into her clothes. As she draws the dressing room curtain closed, she breaks into a sweat and goes limp.

"Right away?" she thinks. "They haven't even done my autopsy, and he's talking about treatment."

"Listen to you," she whispers to herself, "*Biopsy*. Not autopsy!"

Claustrophobic, Julie reopens the curtain and continues the conversation going on in her head. "You thought you beat it, didn't you? After all this time of clean checkups, he's saying it might be back again. And if it is, you'll probably start treatment right away. The cancer cells are probably multiplying out of control. Pop, pop, pop. I think I can hear them!"

With trembling fingers she slips off the paper gown and reaches for her blue shirt, which reminds her of the blue sundress hanging in her closet with the price tag still attached.

"What will I do about Maryanne?" While scurrying to rearrange her schedule to come in today, Julie has been worrying endlessly about her friend's wedding.

Buttoning from the top down, she thinks, "I have a plane ticket to San Francisco. If I'm in treatment, I'll miss it. But I *can't* miss her wedding. I know what I'll do: I'll tell the scheduler that I need to delay."

Holding the bottom button in her fingers, she realizes she's off by one. "No! You can't *tell* them anything, Julie. You'd be marked forever as a 'difficult' patient. Besides, they'd think you're stupid or in denial."

"Okay," Julie answers herself while unbuttoning and re-buttoning, "then I'll *ask* if it's alright to delay. Oh, but that would give the cancer cells a few weeks' head start."

Julie fumbles in her purse for Kleenex. "Now Julie, you know he'll never let you go to California if starting treatment right away will make a difference."

"Yeah. I know," Julie answers herself, bending over her purse and crying softly. The people on the other side of the wall are now quiet, as if they are listening.

"Even if I could magically beam myself to San Francisco for the afternoon, I wouldn't enjoy…" Julie's soliloquy stops mid-thought and she straightens up, as if overtaken by an alter-personality.

"Whoa, hold your horses," the new voice in her head says defiantly. "You are *not*—No, siree—you are *not* letting cancer define your days. Not today; not tomorrow. You *will* find a way to go to California, and you *will* have a great time." She wipes away her tears with the palms of her hands.

Purposefully pulling on her skirt, she thinks. "I'll explain to him about Maryanne's wedding. Surely he will say, 'That's fine, Julie. Go be with your friend.'" Julie zips up too quickly and catches her skin.

"Ouch!" She re-zips. "Is that like, 'Fine, Julie. Go ahead and eat Twinkies instead of fruits and vegetables.'? Is that like, 'Fine, Julie. Cut off your nose...'? Or..." she freezes. "Or does 'fine' mean he expects the treatment won't work this time?" Her hand covers her mouth. "Maybe he wants me to enjoy today, while I can."

"Breathe," she instructs herself and inhales deeply. "Wow, listen to me. I'm having my own little conversation here, aren't I? I'll bet there are men on the other side of this door from the 'Looney Bin,' waiting to take me away."

Julie slips on her shoes and slings her purse over her shoulder. Pulling herself together, she opens the door and heads down the hall toward the appointment clerk. "Whatever the biopsy shows, he'll help me do what's right. He always has."

**

For patients struck by an imminently life-threatening but fixable problem, the choice is easy: Their world stops, and they get off for treatment. In contrast, for patients whose condition is stable, the delayed gratification inherent in difficult treatments can collide with the inspiring notion of "carpe diem"—seize the day.

Physicians are in a unique position to offer guidance and support when the proposed plan of action will keep patients from important duties or deny them rare opportunities. For patients swayed by a sense of urgency not justified by the science, providing a range of acceptable appointment dates when recommending a specific protocol helps them keep things in perspective.

By assuring patients that their scheduling concerns are legitimate—in fact, they indicate a healthy zest for life—and acknowledging the necessary sacrifices, we validate the person beyond the disease.

The act of tailoring schedules to meet patients' needs reminds everyone that the real purpose of treatment is not to add time to lives but to make time for living.

- We build trust by reassuring patients we won't let their desires sway our good judgment.
- By offering a range of appointment dates, we encourage patients to live as fully as possible within the constraints of their illness.
- We validate the value of living joyfully by scheduling medical appointments around patients' activities, when doing so won't compromise their care.

Thanksgiving 2006

One regret about my medical practice still gnaws at me: how I handled gifts. Oh, I always sent nice thank-you notes in a timely manner and refused inappropriately generous gifts. But I was so determined to maintain my objectivity that I never understood what the gifts meant for my patients.

Emma watches me carefully peel the scotch tape off the iridescent paper and unwrap the small white box. With surprise and pleasure, I lift the lid. Then, conscientiously balancing oohs and aahs with you-shouldn't-haves, I slowly remove the delicate teardrop earrings embedded with pale pink pearls from their cottony bed and hold them up to the light.

Emma studies my face to assess how much I like the costume jewelry she picked out. The earbobs are truly lovely; my momentary happiness, genuine. What goes unnoticed (I hope) is the invisible wall rising inside me.

Her gift is unnecessary. Treating her many illnesses is routine in my practice. As for Emma's string of emergency room visits and frequent telephone calls, that just comes with the territory. Her bills are paid; she owes me nothing. Once Emma leaves my office, I quickly close the lid on both the gift and her gratitude.

As a physician, I believe my detachment provides an effective response to patients' thankful praise or presents, just as my professional calm helps me deal with patients' distress or ire.

What's so terrible about basking in patients' gratitude? Why not delight in patients' presents?

Ethicists warn physicians about gift-born bias and clouded clinical judgment. The side effect I fear most is a swelled head. Satiated egos can predispose to medical errors. For the sake of my patients as well as myself, I must guard against expecting or wanting gifts or praise.

My approach to patients' gratitude serves me well. By erecting a wall around my emotions, my affections or concerns for patients won't interfere with my ability to deliver bad news or prescribe risky treatments. Yet I sense something is awry.

Only after I develop cancer do I begin to understand my mistake. Years after receiving her gift, as I experience life on the other side of the stethoscope, I yearn to call Emma. More than wanting to tell her how much pleasure I get from those earrings, I need to talk with her about the ache in my chest.

Ever since my first round of cancer treatment—which began just before Thanksgiving 1990—I've suffered from a recurring discomfort. As predictable as the sunrise, when the leaves turn red and yellow and the days get noticeably shorter, the ache in my chest crescendos until it is almost intolerable.

With our holiday of thanks fast approaching, I wonder if the ache is the swell of gratitude for the medicines and technology (and factors beyond comprehension) that enabled my survival. Or could it be my heightened appreciation for the simple things, a gratitude that nearly explodes inside my chest? If so, why does the sensation persist despite my prayers of thanks and savoring of ordinary moments?

The reason for my discomfort eludes me until my husband, Ted, asks me to proofread his paper on Adam Smith. All I know about Smith is that he was an 18th-century English economist who wrote about self-interest as a driving force in the economy. I didn't realize that Smith was a moral philosopher, too.

Smith believes that benevolence—kindness toward another—acts as a sort of glue that binds individuals together in society. He theorizes that people are wired to respond to kindness with gratitude, and this gratitude compels people to want to return the kindness.

Reading on, Smith's words jump out and resonate with me like a plucked string. In describing the feelings experienced by a recipient of an act of kindness, Smith says (and I'm paraphrasing here): Until I have brought compensation by doing something that promotes their happiness, I feel loaded with a debt that their services have laid upon me.

My doctors and nurses insist I don't owe them anything. Oh, but I do! They have treated me not only with cancer therapies but also with kindness. My gratitude for their kindness builds throughout the season of Thanksgiving, until I find just the right gifts and deliver them in late December.

People nowadays despair that medicine has lost its humanity. Physicians lament that they've become depersonalized mechanics fixing bodies, not people caring for and about other people. But medicine is—and must be—about more than a market exchange of goods and services.

The care of the patient must be built on the same natural human emotions that work in societies as a whole. The exchange of simple kindness, as Smith suggests, is the cement that holds us together.

In my office years ago, my mistake was thinking the pearl earrings were just for me. If I could go back in time, I would open wide my mind and heart whenever a patient thanked me, whether with a gift, a card or simply a hug.

Reveling in patients' gratitude relieves the burden of their debt and nurtures healing alliances. By allowing patients to give thanks and by accepting their thanks, we hold onto that which makes us human.

- We dignify patients by acknowledging their expressions of gratitude.
- We relieve patients of a burden by enjoying their notes and small gifts.
- We find happiness in our work by allowing ourselves to feel appreciated.

Patent Pending

"Patent pending" is slang among clinicians for "morbidly obese." In the care of a patient who is grieving the premature loss of a loved one, "patent pending" takes on a new meaning, conjuring a healing image.

"So young!" I cry. It feels too soon. A life cut short. How could this be?

The teacher nods sympathetically and then drops a hint, "Your measurement is wrong."

"*You're* wrong!" I think to myself, trying to hide my anger. My numbers add up perfectly, every way I count them. I can calculate to the minute. To the second, if you like. I think longingly of all the days that he might have had, the dreams now gone forever. "I'm sure my numbers are accurate," I say, my veneer of calm slipping. "Which is why it's not fair. Not right. Surely, a mistake."

The teacher once again nods, "Your readings are correct, but look at your yardstick."

"My ruler?" Suddenly I remember an afternoon in my youth when the world was a wonder and I was thirsty. I demanded the tall slender glass, absolutely sure it held more juice. When handed the stubby tumbler, I was furious. "I got less," I protested. "It's not fair!"

So my mother poured the contents of each glass into side-by-side identical measuring cups. At first, I thought it was a trick. Or magic. Then I saw I was wrong. Just as the difference in height of the orange menisci had disappeared, so, too, did my anger. I was once again happy, my thirst quenched. And thereafter I knew: My mind can deceive me if I use the wrong measuring tool.

"So how does one measure a life?" I ask.

"Not by how many, how quickly, how far. Not by how much," the teacher answers.

"Then, how?" I ask.

"Yes. How."

"How?" I repeat.

"What matters is not *what* one does, but *how*. With purpose? With loving kindness?"

"Can I know the heart of someone who is gone? I ask. "If so, how?"

"By focusing on the imprint in the sand or the ripple in the pond."

"I don't understand."

"When an artist is done, do you measure how much paint is on the canvas or how long it took to put it there? Do you add up the notes of a score or the words in a book? Stop counting the number of nails the carpenter used and stop looking for the price tag on the curtains if you want to see the home in the house."

I'm beginning to see that mournful measuring can lead me away from truth into anger or despair. "So please tell me," I yearn to know, "the reproducible irreducible measure of a life. Is there such a thing?"

"You want a unit, like an inch or a pound?"

"I want to know the measure of a life."

"I told you that one way to measure is by looking at what's left behind. There are other ways, but they all require faith."

"Faith?" I ask.

"You must believe—have trust—in measures that are unlike inches or pounds. And then you can know."

"What other measures?"

"A measure that convinces you Picasso's Dove, created with but one deft brush stroke, and Michelangelo's meticulously painted Sistine Chapel are both masterpieces. A measure that assures you an 8-year-old child's Haiku is as complete as *Moby Dick*. A baby's giggle? As glorious as Beethoven's *Ode to Joy*."

"Does this measure count heroism?" I ask. Or quiet acts of fortitude? Generosity? Honor? Duty? Beauty? Does this measure weigh in love?"

"A single kiss can be eternal. But beware: All that glitters is not gold. Measure wisely and you won't be fooled."

My desire for a measure reminds me of a time when I was a doctor and needed an exact weight of one of my patients. I can still see my old office scale—the stand-up kind whose big round face had numbers around the edge except at 12 o'clock, where two words marked the spot. I can still picture my patient lumbering onto its platform, his weight far exceeding capacity and forcing me to look elsewhere for my answer.

Yesteryear's exasperation is today's comfort: Were my friend to step on a scale-of-life, he would surely, as did my patient, send the needle spinning wildly—once, twice—before it slowed down to a stop, the tip of the arrow pointing to "Patent Pending."

- We help patients heal by listening to their grieving.
- We bring patients comfort by helping them reframe losses.
- We encourage patients to embrace life by helping them hope for a time when the memories of loved ones serve as blessings in their lives.

Epilogue

We've reached the end of my stories. My 10 seconds are up. Now you can grab your stethoscope and jump back into the pressure-cooker we call modern medicine. Some days I wonder how you do it.

Your work puts more demands on you than when I practiced medicine. Just look at the changes that have taken place over the past decade. You routinely order tests and therapies that your patients undergo far from the warmth of your office. You field endless questions from Internet-informed—and misinformed—patients who want detailed answers. Add to that the drudgery of convoluted billing codes and mountains of insurance forms, as well as the financial stresses of rising overhead costs and declining reimbursements. I can see how difficult it is to find the time needed for compassionate care.

Meanwhile, in the comfort of my home I've been writing about clinician-patient relationships. Removed from the stresses and strains of the clinic and hospital, it would be easy for me to slip into armchair philosophizing about how to deliver medical care. Believe me, telling any clinician how to do his or her work has never been my intention. Quite the contrary. As I said, some days I wonder how you do it.

I wrote this book to offer you a creative way to escape the pressures of your daily work, whether for a few hours or just a few minutes. I hope these stories helped you take a step back, reflect on your work and, maybe, enjoy a laugh or two. If you now understand your patients a little better or have more confidence in how you can help them, that's good. Of course nothing would thrill me more than if you can't wait to return to work, energized by a renewed sense of purpose—that intoxicating blend of desire and determination that drove you to choose medicine as a career.

Since at least the time of Hippocrates, the practice of medicine has been an art based on science. Despite all the changes of our modern age pulling you farther and farther away from your patients, healing still begins the moment you use words or touch to make contact with your patients. And I believe that no matter how clinical practice changes in the future, the heart of medicine will always lie deep within the clinician-patient bond.

I have hope for our future. I envision a restructured healthcare system in which our science supports, not replaces, our art. As long as we keep thinking and talking about our shared mission of healing others, it can happen. Until then, I'll leave you with the words of Maimonides, "May the love of your art inspire your work."

Glossary

ALS   amyotrophic lateral sclerosis, also known as Lou Gehrig's disease; a neuromuscular disease marked by progressive weakness leading to death

Algorithm   a set of steps used in diagnosing and treating a disease

Analgesic   a drug that relieves or allays pain; (adj.) pertaining to pain relief

Attending physician   consulting physician; staff physician; physician who has completed all of his or her training

CHF   congestive heart failure; a weakness of the heart that causes fluid to back up into the lungs

Diagnosis   the act or process of identifying or determining the nature and cause of a disease or injury through evaluation

14-18 chromosomal translocation   the most common chromosomal abnormality found in cancer cells of patients with follicular non-Hodgkin's lymphoma; specific switching of small pieces of DNA between chromosome #14 and chromosome #18

History   the facts of the case; the patient's description of symptoms, past medical problems, family illnesses, social factors

Gluteal   pertaining to the buttocks

Guaiac test   a test for blood in urine or feces using a reagent containing guaiacum that yields a blue color when blood is present

H&P   medical history and physical exam

Indolent   slow-growing

Interferons   natural proteins produced by the cells of the immune system of most vertebrates in response to challenges by foreign agents such as viruses, parasites, and tumor cells

Intern staff physician; usually a recent graduate of medical school receiving post-graduate training who is supervised by more-experienced staff members

Latent syphilis stage of syphilis when patient has proof of infection but no symptoms

Lymphoma cancer that begins in the lymphocytes of the immune system (lymph nodes, spleen, thymus)

MI myocardial infarction; heart attack

Neuropathic arising from disease or disorder of the nervous system

Neurosyphilis syphilis that has infected the brain or spinal cord

Oncologist physician who specializes in the diagnosis and treatment of cancer

Palliative care medical care devoted to reducing the severity of symptoms rather than giving treatments intended to cure or slow the progression of disease

PDR Physicians' Desk Reference; reference volume containing full information on prescription and over-the-counter drugs

Plenary panel conference panel whose discussion is geared to all attendees

Prognosis prediction of course or end of disease; estimate of chance for recovery

Puerperal fever bacterial infection occurring primarily in women after delivering a baby

Recurrence return of disease or symptoms after period of remission or quiescence

Remission lessening of symptoms or evidence of disease; in the setting of cancer, used colloquially to mean "complete remission," namely, no evidence of disease.

Salvage therapies treatments given when disease does not respond to standard therapies; treatments of last resort

Sigmoidoscopy internal examination of the lower colon using a sigmoidoscope

Subcutaneous under the skin

VDRL venereal disease research laboratory test; VDRL is a screening test for syphilis that measures antibodies that can be produced by *Treponema pallidum*, the bacteria that causes syphilis

About the Author

Wendy S. Harpham, MD, FACP, is a doctor of internal medicine, survivor of chronic indolent lymphoma, wife and mother of three. Her writing has been honored with numerous local and national awards, including the 2000 Governor's Award, for which she was inducted into the Texas Women's Hall of Fame.

In addition to her writing, Dr Harpham has become a nationally recognized speaker for professional and lay audiences. She devotes her energy to helping survivors directly through her writing and speaking, and indirectly through her activities as a patient advocate. Limited stamina prevents her from returning to clinical medicine at this time.

Website: www.wendyharpham.com
Blog: www.wendyharpham.typepad.com